Advance Praise for *John Piper, Calvinism, and Missions*

While in seminary, as part of a special missions course, I went on an oversees mission trip with some of my fellow students, and we were assigned Let the Nations be Glad by John Piper. We read various other books, but Piper's work stood out for a number of reasons, including the fact that he wrote from a robustly reformed perspective. This work sparked all sorts of conversations among our group. Doesn't a Calvinistic belief in divine election stifle extinguish missional motivation? In this important work, Dr. Hopkins explores the relationship between Piper's theology and missiology. Writing as a seasoned missionary with the mind of a theologian, Hopkins has made a significant contribution to the field of missiology. This book will benefit not just those in the academic world, but also boots on the ground Christians who want to see the nations be glad and rejoice in our Savior.

Tony Merida
Founding Pastor, Imago Dei Church, Raleigh, NC

With a professor's precision and a missionary's passion, Phil Hopkins takes on the age-old questions about how Calvinism and missions are related. He does this through the biographical lens of studying John Piper, a reformed pastor who has influenced thousands of other leaders to be intentionally on mission because of

– not in spite of - those doctrinal convictions. Theology and missiology are joined in this volume which will stimulate your mind
and invigorate your passion for God's glory to be demonstrated by
God's eternal mission.

Jeff Iorg
President, SBC Executive Committee

About this Book

John Piper has been a key figure in Reformed theology for decades, and he continues to influence many. But how can Christian missions be accommodated with predestination?

This book explores the relationship between Calvinism and missions, using John Piper as a case study. It examines how Piper reconciles the doctrines of Calvinism, which emphasize God's sovereignty and predestination, with a commitment to missions and evangelism.

The author discusses Piper's background, influences, and theological development, highlighting events and people who shaped his understanding of missions. Piper's belief in Christian Hedonism, which emphasizes the pursuit of everlasting pleasures that honor God, is presented as a foundational principle that motivates and dictates his missiology.

The book delves into Piper's understanding of God's will and explores the concept of God having more than one way of willing. This concept allows Piper to reconcile God's universal love and desire for all people to be saved with His electing love and predestination of some. The author also defines key terms related to Calvinism and missions to provide clarity and context.

The book aims to shed light on Piper's internal consistency in his theological thought and to evaluate how his understanding of God's glory motivates and dictates his missiology. It is aimed at an audience that is well-informed regarding theology.

Philip O. Hopkins is a religious historian with a special interest in missions. He has PhD degrees from Southeastern Baptist Theological Seminary (Applied Theology) and from the University of St. Andrews (Iranian History). He spent nearly 20 years analying ethnic and minority peoples in Iran, Turkey, and the Caucasus region. He is now Professor of Missions at Gateway Seminary. He lives in southern California with his wife, Mary Ann. They have one son.

John Piper, Calvinism, and Missions

A Way Forward

Philip O. Hopkins

Energion Publications
Cantonment, Florida
2024

ISBN: 978-1-63199-914-7
eISBN: 978-1-63199-915-4
Library of Congress Control Number: 2024947125

Energion Publications
1241 Conference Rd.
Cantonment, FL 32533

(850) 525-3916
energion.com
pubs@energion.com

To
My Mom

Nancy P. Hopkins

for her love for family and desire to see people come to
Christ. She has exemplified faith in God during challenges not
meant for only one person to bear.

TABLE OF CONTENTS

Acknowledgments

The work is a revision of my dissertation completed in 2005 and *God's Desire for the Nations* written in 2010. There are several people that deserve special recognition for helping me. My wife, Mary Ann, not only encouraged me to finish this work, but also a second PhD. She exhibits the qualities of a wife mentioned in Prov 31:10–31 and 1 Pet 3:4. I have not only a soulmate but also a partner in ministry who loves God with all her heart, mind, and soul. I thank my younger brother, his family, and my mom, and grandmother. Their trust in God's sweet sovereignty in all situations, including during times of death, is a testimony to their faith in Christ and is an example to us all. Philip F. Hopkins, my father, who died unexpectedly during the dissertation's completion, worked tirelessly to see people in New England come to faith in Christ. My son, Sam, now entering his pre-teen years, is a joy to be around. Until the last few months, outside of being born in the United States, he has never lived in America; his insights are helping us with reverse culture shock.

Additional thanks to the late Howard F. Vos, Keith E. Eitel, and John S. Hammett. Vos' constant encouragement and push for perfection during my college years made me realize that God requires your best effort, which is far beyond what seems capable at the time. Eitel's requirement of *Let the Nations Be Glad!* in his introductory missions class introduced me to John Piper. Hammett's God-centered understanding of theology along with his Christ-like humility spurred me to think on deeper theological issues.

Ali M. Ansari, Garnik Asatrian, and Victoria Arakelova need mentioning as well. Ansari's push to write and research critically and academically – like a historian – is cherished. I value his insights and friendship. Asatrian and Arakelova spurred my love for Armenia and Iran, two of the harder places to reach people for Christ. Armenia will always be on our hearts. Lord willing, the conflicts with Azerbaijan and Artsakh and Turkey and the Armenian Genocide will be resolved peacefully in my lifetime.

Now I am in my 50s. Nearly 20 years of living overseas, another PhD, a professorship, and an unexpected return to the United States have challenged my thoughts and refined my thinking. To the people I have met along the way – Christian and non-Christian – I am grateful.

My family and I will always have a love for Iran and the Iranian people. We have learned more about hospitality and love for people from Iranians than from any other group. If we could live anywhere in the world, we would live in Iran. Iran's people, culture, and way of life make us long for the day when the hostility between our two countries ends.

PREFACE

During my time in seminary, I was taught that Calvinism hindered missions. One could not be a consistent Calvinist and be missions minded at the same time. Calvinists who were missions minded were like mules, unable or rarely able to reproduce. I wanted to explore this idea in detail as missionaries from William Carey and Adoniram Judson onward (and beforehand) had sympathies or were proponents of the Doctrines of Grace. I also wanted to honor my professors and not cause any undue trouble. I thought a PhD would be an effective way to clarify my thoughts and give my professors an opportunity to challenge my thinking. With John Piper, a pastor, writer, and former professor then growing in popularity – one who openly endorsed both Calvinism and missions – I thought he would be a good test case. Why – or how – could he be both ... at least in his own mind? If I could figure out how Piper squared these ideas – even in conflict – that would help me as I had a similar struggle.

I am not seeking to defend Piper's interpretation. I am not stating I agree with it; I am not stating I do not, either. Instead, I want to explain how Piper can be both a Calvinist and missions minded. I am seeking to see whether Piper is internally consistent in his thought – especially since he has been in some type of ministry for over a half century – and whether Piper's understanding of God's glory seen through Calvinism motivates and dictates his missiology and understanding of missions.

I have done my best to make this edition more readable. Chapters are shortened, footnotes are abbreviated, and first and second person are used. Nonetheless, its original form was a PhD dissertation and still reads "PhD-ish." For those used to reading popular works, this book might be a bit more challenging. For those used to reading scholarly pieces, they might be disappointed.

1

WHY JOHN PIPER?

WHO IS JOHN PIPER?

John Piper has been a household name for over a generation, but at the time of drafting the dissertation, he was not. One of the reasons for Piper's increasing in popularity was the work *Let the Nations Be Glad!*, now a perennial best seller that has been read by countless missionaries, pastors, and seminary students. It has been translated into a number of languages, including Farsi, the language Iranians speak. Piper's desire for us to understand that God is glorified and we are satisfied when we glorify God by "enjoying him forever"[1] – Christian Hedonism – challenges us to pursue everlasting pleasures that honor God, which is practically lived out in a Calvinist understanding of cross-cultural evangelism.

For the rest of this chapter, I want to (re)introduce Piper, starting with the events and people who influenced him. From there I will present the idea of God having more than one way of willing, which is how Piper reconciles God's universal love with God's electing love. To state this another way, God having more than one way of willing is how Piper marries Calvinism and missions. This chapter will end with some terms that need to be defined.

---

1   John Piper, *Desiring God: Meditations of a Christian Hedonist*, 3d ed. (Sisters, OR: Multnomah, 2003), 17.

EVENTS SHAPING PIPER'S UNDERSTANDING OF MISSIONS[2]

John Stephen Piper was born on January 11, 1946, in Chattanooga, Tennessee. He lived most of his childhood and youth in Greenville, South Carolina, where his father, an itinerant evangelist, and mother, a housewife, stressed biblical teaching in the home. At the age of six, he became a Christian and later was baptized.[3] At the age of twenty-two, he married Noel Henry.[4] They have five children: Karsten Luke, Benjamin John, Abraham Christian, Barnabas William, and Talitha Ruth,[5] and several grandchildren.

During the summer between his sophomore and junior year at Wheaton College, Piper sensed a call to the "ministry of the Word."[6] This call led him to pursue a Master of Divinity degree at Fuller Theological Seminary. At Fuller, three notable events unfolded: he met Daniel Fuller, "the most influential living teacher of his life;" he was introduced to Jonathan Edwards' writings, "the most influential dead teacher in his life;" and he became convinced of the truths of Calvinism. Upon graduation, Piper pursued a doctorate in New Testament at the University of Munich in West Germany (1971–74), followed by a six-year professorship at

2   This section gleans heavily from two sources: "Biography of John Piper," <http://www.desiringgod.org/who_is_dgm/about_piper/piper_bio. html>, site editor, Desiring God Ministries, accessed on 10 April 2003; and John Piper, "The Absolute Sovereignty of God," <http://desiringgod. org/library/sermons/02/ 110302.html>, site editor, Desiring God Ministries, November 3, 2002, accessed on 24 April 2003.

3   John Piper, "The Author of the Greatest Letter Ever Written," <http:// www.desiringgod.org/library/sermons/98/042698.html>, site editor, Desiring God Ministries, April 26, 1998, accessed on 8 May 2003.

4   John Piper, "Thirty Stanzas," <http://www.desiringgod.org/library/ poems/98/thirty_ stanzas.html>, site editor, Desiring God Ministries, December 21, 1998, accessed on 15 May 2003.

5   John Piper, *The Pleasures of God The Pleasures of God: Meditations on God's Delight in Being God*, rev. and expanded ed. (Sisters, OR: Multnomah, 2000), 14.

6   Piper, "The Author of the Greatest Letter Ever Written."

Bethel College in St. Paul, Minnesota. While on sabbatical examining Rom 9:1–23, his call to the "ministry of the Word" shifted from collegiate teaching to the pastorate. He resigned his teaching position, and Bethlehem Baptist Church in Minneapolis, Minnesota, called him soon after to be pastor. He ministered there from 1980 until his retirement in 2013.

Piper states that the urgency of missions did not mature until he preached a sermon entitled, "Missions: The Battle Cry of Christian Hedonism," in the fall of 1983. He states that after the sermon he and other leaders at Bethlehem believed "a new calling" for the church had arisen "toward the unfinished task of reaching the unreached peoples [for Christ]."[7] Since then, Piper's passion for God's glory seen in Calvinism and missions have been inseparable.[8] Even now, as Piper has been retired for a decade, his passion for Calvinism and missions has remained.[9]

---

7   John Piper, "Let the Nations Be Glad!," <http://www.desiringgod.org/library/sermons/93/110793.html>, site editor, Desiring God Ministries, November 7, 1993, accessed on 14 May 2003.

8   John Piper to Philip O. Hopkins, 21 December 2004, transcript in hand of Philip O. Hopkins, Special Collections. Piper recognizes that his Calvinism was not completely biblical before 1983. He states his theology may not be completely biblical at the present; to know and understand God is part of the sanctification process. Piper also credits becoming a pastor in aiding his missions motivation. He equates becoming a pastor to becoming a parent. The parent not only has to teach his children what is important, he also has to model it. In relation to missions he states, "Good grief, look, this entire people are looking at me to see what is important in life. I better get real serious about the universe and the nations."

9   For example, there are several Piper sermons on the Desiring God website that occur after his retirement on missions. See: "Frontier Missions," <https://www.desiringgod.org/topics/frontier-missions/messages>, site editor, Desiring God Ministries, April 22, 1990, accessed on 31 January 2024.

PEOPLE SHAPING PIPER'S THOUGHT

Piper's Parents

Piper does not remember much of his theological roots.[10] He does recognize that his parents had a strong Christian faith[11] and taught their children Scripture in family devotionals.[12] He credits his mother for teaching him how to pray,[13] and for his belief in God, as she served as an example of a "good 'God'" to him.[14] His father, an itinerant evangelist who was away two-thirds of the time,[15] provided him a unique understanding of the sacrifice needed to proclaim the gospel. His father taught him never to "be above" personal evangelism. [16] The roots of John Piper's concept of the glory of God also came from his father who mentioned God's glory in the home. In interviewing William Piper, he stated that everything Christians do "should be for the glory of God."[17] William Piper taught and lived out passages like Ps 90:14,[18] which emphasizes the now popular theme that his son often promotes:

---

10   John Piper: In Retirement of William Piper, prod., Rogma 1998, 120 min, Special Collections videocassette.

11   John Piper, "The Lord Stood by Me," <http://www.desiringgod.org/ library/sermons/90/042290.html>, site editor, Desiring God Ministries, April 22, 1990, accessed on 17 June 2003.

12   William Piper, John Piper's late father and former President of Rogma International, interview by author, 07 July 2003, Easley, South Carolina. See: http://www.rogma.org/index.htm.

13   John Piper, "Raising Children Who Hope in the Triumph of God," <http://www.desiringgod.org/library/sermons/88/050888.html>, site editor, Desiring God Ministries, May 8, 1988, accessed on 17 June 2003.

14   John Piper, "Thankful for the Love of God! Why?," <http://www.desiringgod.org/library/sermons/01/111801.html> site editor, Desiring God Ministries, November 18, 2001, accessed on 17 June 2003.

15   John Piper, "Holy Women Who Hoped in God," <http://www.desiringgod.org/library/sermons/86/051186.html>, site editor, Desiring God Ministries, May 11, 1986, accessed on 17 June 2003.

16   Piper, Retirement of William Piper.

17   William Piper interview.

18   Ibid.

"God is most glorified in us when we are most satisfied in him."
Whenever John Piper rereads his father's works, it reminds him
again that the theme of God's glory in many of his own books
arose from his father's influence.[19]

Daniel Fuller

While Piper's parents influenced him in the home, Fuller
taught Piper hermeneutics, helped to develop his understanding
of God's glory, and introduced him to the writings of Jonathan
Edwards. Piper states his debt to Fuller is "incalculable," and calls
him his hero and mentor.[20] In Fuller's class on hermeneutics, he
explained that the Bible depicts God creating for the delight of his
glory.[21] Piper states that the class "opened a window on a world of
glory that has never been shut."[22] Fuller's approach helped Piper
see that the glory of God and the ultimate joy of people are the
same.[23] In Fuller's *Unity of the Bible: Unfolding God's Plan for Humanity*, a book that summarized his class on hermeneutics, he out-
lined his method. He challenged students to judge their interpretation of the Bible using the inductive method[24] and find support
in relevant historical and textual material.[25] Piper states this work
influenced him more than any other book outside the Bible.[26] In

---

19   Piper, Retirement of William Piper.

20   John Piper, *Don't Waste Your Life* (Wheaton, IL: Crossway, 2003), 26,
     28; John Piper, "The Greatest of These Is Love: Summer Is for See-
     ing and Showing Christ," <http://www.desiringgod.org/library/ser-
     mons/95/061195.html>, site editor, Desiring God Ministries, June 11,
     1995, accessed on 16 July 2003; and Piper, Desiring God, 13.

21   Daniel Fuller, *Unity of the Bible: Unfolding God's Plan for Humanity*
     (Grand Rapids: Zondervan, 1991), xiv.

22   John Piper, *God's Passion for His Glory: Living the Vision of Jonathan
     Edwards* (Wheaton, IL: Crossway, 1998), xvi n 1, states that *The Unity of
     the Bible* was the "published fruits" of the class.

23   Ibid., 32.

24   Ibid., xvii–xviii.

25   Fuller, *Unity of the Bible*, 110–11.

26   John Piper, "Foreword," in Fuller, *Unity of the Bible*, x.

Desiring God, Piper states clearly Fuller's impact: "It was his class in 1968 where the seminal discoveries were made. It was from him that I learned to dig for gold rather than to rake for leaves when I take up the Scriptures."[27]

C. S. Lewis

Lewis influenced Piper's ideas about being happy in God, which is essential for Christians to worship God. Lewis' influence led him to adopt the principles of Christian Hedonism.[28] Piper remarks that Lewis clarified that the desire to be happy is not bad. Lewis believed that the problem is that people do not seek enough pleasure. In this regard, Piper quotes Lewis in another now popular phrase. People are:

> half-hearted creatures, fooling about with drink and sex and ambition when infinite joy is offered us, like an ignorant child who wants to go on making mud pies in a slum because he cannot imagine what is meant by the offer of a holiday at the sea. We are far too easily pleased.[29]

Piper comments that Lewis states happiness should instinctively and automatically stream into praise.[30] Our duty as Christians is to be as happy as possible[31] because praising God not only conveys happiness, it is its goal.[32]

---

27 Piper, *Desiring God*, 13. In the second edition of Desiring God, 11, the impact of Fuller's influence is greater. He states, "As with almost everything I do, the influence of Daniel P. Fuller pervades. It was his class in 1968 where the seminal discoveries were made. I would be happy to view this book as explanation and application of his great book, *Unity of the Bible* (Zondervan, 1992)."

28 Piper, *Desiring God*, 22.

29 C. S. Lewis, *The Weight of Glory and Other Addresses* (Grand Rapids: Eerdmans, 1965), 1–2; quoted in Piper, *Desiring God*, 20.

30 C. S. Lewis, *Reflections on the Psalms* (New York: Harcourt, Brace & World, 1958), 94–95; quoted in Piper, *Desiring God*, 22.

31 Piper, *Desiring God*, 94.

32 Ibid., 22.

Jonathan Edwards

Perhaps no one has influenced Piper more than Edwards. Fuller introduced Piper to him when he required his students to read *The End for Which God Created the World*. Since that reading, Piper's theology has been influenced by Edwards' understanding of the glory of God.[33] Piper states that Edwards is the "compass of my theological studies,"[34] especially, *The End for Which God Created the World*, which has "put its stamp on every part of my life and ministry."[35]

Edwards, like Fuller and like Lewis, believed God's glory and our good are the same. Edwards states, "God is glorified not only by His glory being seen, but by its being rejoiced in. . . . God made the world that He might communicate, and the creature receive, His glory; and that it might [be] received both by the mind and heart."[36] Piper explains that *The Freedom of the Will*, that God's sovereignty over humans' will "cements the truth of [his] supremacy in all things for the joy of all peoples."[37]

Piper describes several "implications" of Edwards' understanding of God's glory that relate to missions. First, God's righteousness does not contradict his mercy. In Christ's death, God simultaneously upheld his righteousness, his "commitment to his glory," and cleansed sinners by his mercy, his "commitment to our

---

33　John Piper, "The Pastor as Theologian: Reflections on the Ministry of Jonathan Edwards," <http://desiringgod.org/library/ biographies/88edwards.html>, site editor, Desiring God Ministries, April 15, 1988, accessed on 15 May 2003.

34　Piper, "The Pastor as Theologian: Reflections on the Ministry of Jonathan Edwards."

35　John Piper, *God's Passion for His Glory: Living the Vision of Jonathan Edwards* (Wheaton, IL: Crossway, 1998), 31.

36　Jonathan Edwards, quoted in John Piper, "A Mind in Love with God: The Private Life of a Modern Evangelical," <http://desiringgod.org/ library/topics/edwards/edwards_mind.html>, site editor, Desiring God Ministries, July 1 997, accessed on 1 5 May 2003.

37　Jonathan Edwards, *Freedom of the Will*, ed. Paul Ramsey (New Haven: Yale University Press, 1957), 89.

joy." Second, God's glory is the only thing that will satisfy the soul. All genuinely loving or virtuous acts by Christians should aim to bring people to "rejoice in the glory of God." Third, evangelism must demonstrate Christ's beauty and salvific work with a "heartfelt urgency of love that labors to help people find their satisfaction in him." Fourth, missions is professing God's glory among the unreached people groups with the intent to gather God's children.[38] These implications play a role in how Piper understands missions, which will be seen in later in the book.

Other People Who Have Influenced Piper

Aside from the people mentioned there are others who have impacted Piper's thought.[39] Six of them need a brief mention: Blaise Pascal, E. D. Hirsch, Jr., Mortimer Adler George Ladd, and David and Faith Jaeger. The writings of Pascal, along with Lewis, introduced Piper to one of his most important ideas seen in Christian Hedonism: all people seek happiness, and seeking happiness is not wrong. Piper incorporated Pascal's belief that while people may seek after worldly pleasure, only God can satisfy human being's desire.[40] The works of Hirsch and Adler influenced Piper on interpretation and gaining understanding from books, respectively. Hirsch explained that the meaning of a work is objec-

---

38   Ibid., 33–42.

39   Piper lists others who have influenced him such as: Stephen Charnock, Ian Murray, Thomas Watson, John Owen, Martin Lloyd Jones, Charles Spurgeon, and Augustine. See John Piper, "Books that Have Influenced Me the Most," <http://www.desiringgod.org/library/topics/leadership/books.html>, site editor, Desiring God Ministries, November 1993, accessed on 6 August 2003; "What Books Have Been Most Influential in John Piper's Life and Thought?," <http://www.desiringgod.org/ who_ is_dgm/about_piper/ books. html>, site editor, Desiring God Ministries, accessed on 6 August 2003; and "What Ideas Have Strongly Influenced John Piper?," <http://www.desiringgod.org/who_ is_dgm/about_ piper/ ideas.html>, site editor, Desiring God Ministries, accessed on 6 August 2003.

40   Blaise Pascal, *Pascal's Pensees*, trans. W. F. Trotter (NY: E. P. Dutton, 1958), 113; in Piper, *Desiring God*, 19.

tive; meaning is outside of the reader. Adler encouraged reading works that are harder to understand to develop sounder reasoning skills.[41] Ladd impacted his understanding of New Testament theology, especially redemptive history.[42] The Jaegers, missionaries to Africa from Bethlehem Baptist Church, encouraged Piper to become active in missions. Piper even took a six-week trip to see them in 1985.[43]

INTRODUCTION TO THE IDEA THAT GOD HAS MORE THAN ONE WAY OF WILLING

Piper believes that God glorifies himself in missions through unconditionally electing individuals to salvation. Piper's understanding of God's secret will, his understanding of election and electing love, and his belief that the Christian must share the gospel to all nations are seen particularly in his understanding of the doctrine of election and Christian Hedonism. Piper states that the "essential nature" of God is "to dispense mercy . . . on whomever he pleases, apart from any constraint originating outside his [a person's] own will."[44] Piper stresses that God elects individuals to salvation to proclaim his name. Salvation comes by faith through the preaching of the gospel, but God is the one who converts, effectually calls, and gathers.[45] God raises the spiritually dead and gives them life.[46]

Piper also believes that God glorifies himself in missions through universal love. He states that God's "righteousness demands that He be a God of love . . . love is at the very heart of God's being."[47] God's universal love is seen especially in his

41   Piper, "Books that Have Influenced Me the Most."
42   Ibid.
43   Piper, Letter to Philip O. Hopkins.
44   John Piper, *The Justification of God: An Exegetical and Theological Study of Romans 9:1–23*, 2d ed. (Grand Rapids: Baker, 2001), 219.
45   John Piper, *The Pleasures of God: Meditations on God's Delight in Being God*, rev. and expanded ed. (Sisters, OR: Multnomah, 2000), 132.
46   Piper, Desiring God, 235.
47   John Piper, "Brothers, God is Love!," <http://www.desiringgod.org/

revealed will, where God's desire to save the nations is evident. Piper's understanding of God's revealed will, his understanding of God's universal love for people, and his belief that the Christian must share the gospel to all people groups are seen especially in his conception of common grace. In a sermon on Rom 10:1, Piper comments that because God sorrows over the damnation of unbelievers, Christians should act.[48] Since God calls all men to place faith in Christ,[49] believers need to share the gospel.

In Piper's understanding of the glory of God in salvation, which involves a combination of individual, unconditional election with universal love, he reconciles the two seemingly opposing emphases of particularity and universality with the promotion of what I like to call the "Two Wills of God Thesis."[50] Piper distinguishes between what God "would like to see happen" and what God "wills to happen."[51] God has a revealed will and a secret will; he desires to save all (revealed will), while he elects individuals unconditionally (secret will) apart from any action taken by them.[52]

DEFINITION OF TERMS

When Piper uses the term "missions," he distinguishes it from evangelism. He believes evangelism is the proclamation of the gospel in one's own culture. He sees evangelism as types of, "domestic ministries," which include sharing the gospel in min-

---

library/topics/leadership/brothers_godislove.html>, site editor, Desiring God Ministries, accessed on 13 March 2003.

48 John Piper, "Heart's Desire," <http://www.desiringgod.org/library/sermons/85/ 010685.html>, site editor, Desiring God Ministries, January 6, 1985, accessed on 24 February 2003.

49 John Piper, "The Duty: Faith," <http://desiringgod.org/library/sermons/94/121894.html>, site editor, Desiring God Ministries, December 18,1994, accessed on 13 March 2003.

50 The "Two wills of God" is short for two distinct, but not separate wills in the one will of God. Piper does not use the term; it is a way to summarize Piper's understanding.

51 Piper, *The Pleasures of God*, 319.

52 Ibid., 313–40.

istering to the poor, fighting against abortion, door-to-door witnessing, and teaching children's Sunday School.[53] He understands missions as the proclamation of the gospel in a culture other than one's own.[54] He divides missions into "Timothy-type" missions and "Paul-type" missions or frontier missions. Timothy-type missions consists of cross-cultural evangelism among reached people groups.[55] Paul-type missions consists of cross-cultural evangelism among unreached people groups.[56] Piper states that Paul-type missions is imperative and indispensable.[57] Unreached people groups are Piper's priority in missions.

Piper explains the importance of Paul-type missions in an illustration of two sinking ocean liners. There is a rescue attempt, but there are not enough lifeboats to save all the passengers. In the ocean liner farthest from the lifeboats, the passengers are intoxicated, making the rescue more difficult. Piper believes passengers from both ocean liners must be saved though more lives may be lost by going to the farthest boat. The goal for missions is similar: to "win"[58] or reach as many people as possible from all peoples,

---

53   John Piper, "The Relationship Between Diversified Domestic Ministries and Frontier Missions," <http://www.desiringgod.org/library/sermons/84/111884.html>, site editor, Desiring God Ministries, November 18, 1984, accessed on 1 March 2004.

54   Piper, *Desiring God*, 229.

55   John Piper and Tom Steller, "Driving Convictions Behind World Missions at Bethlehem," <http://bbcmpls.org>, site editor, Bethlehem Baptist Church, 1996, accessed on 1 March 2004.

56   John Piper, "Missions and the End of History," <http://www.desiringgod.org/library/sermons/97/102697.html> , site editor, Desiring God Ministries, October 26, 1997, accessed on 1 March 2004.

57   John Piper, "The Revelation of God's Righteousness Where There Is No Church," <http://www.desiringgod.org/library/sermons/99/110799.html>, site editor, Desiring God Ministries, November 7, 1999, accessed on 1 March 2004.

58   Joseph M. Stovall, in *John Piper, Let the Nations Be Glad! The Supremacy of God in Missions*, 2d ed. (Grand Rapids: Baker, 2003), 157 n 1, uses the idea of "win" in the context of save in 1 Cor 9:19–22: "to be used by God in love and witness to win people over to faith in Christ and so save them from sin and condemnation."

including peoples who severely misunderstand and reject Christ.[59] When Piper refers to the term "missions," without any reference to what kind of missions, normally he means Paul-type of missions.[60]

Piper understands that the imprecise nature of the terms "people group" and "unreached" leads to an ambiguous definition of missions.[61] There are many types of people groups mentioned in Scripture, most notably: tongues, tribes, peoples, nations, and families, seen in passages such as Rev 5:9, 7:9, and Gen 12:1–3.[62] Language distinguishes these groups, but the biblical understanding of language is unclear. Further, the terms "people" and "nation" are almost indistinguishable from one another.[63] As well, there is uncertainty to the exact nature of the term "family." A family is larger than a household, but smaller than a tribe; different families may use the same language.[64] Piper states that Scripture purposely

---

59   Ibid., 155–57.

60   Piper, *Desiring God*, 226.

61   Jim Reapsome, "People Groups: Beyond the Push to Reach Them Lie Some Contrary Opinions," *Evangelical Missions Quarterly 20* (January 1984): 6–19, discusses a variety of interpretations and critiques the terms "people groups" and "unreached."

62   Piper, *Let the Nations Be Glad!*, 167–70, states Peter and Paul both cite Gen 12:1–3. Peter cites this promise in Acts 3:25, but uses the word *patriai*, another term for people group or clan instead of *phylai*. Paul quotes the same promise in Gal 3:6–8 but uses the phrase *ta ethné* instead of *phylai*. The phrase *ta ethné* is used twice in the passage, once to refer to individuals and once to refer to people groups. Piper explains that this emphasizes the occurrence of salvation will occur among individuals from all people groups, and, that in this instance, nations (*ta ethné*) designate small bodies of ethnically related people, such as clans.

63   Piper, *Let the Nations Be Glad!*, 188–90. This is one reason why experts disagree in numbering people groups. Piper cites Ralph Winter and Patrick Johnstone and David Barrett who provide vastly different statistics. Winter/Johnson believe there are 24,000 people groups and Barrett maintains there are 12,000 people groups. They disagree because they understand the term "language" differently.

64   Piper, *Let the Nations Be Glad!*, 190–91, 194

has not given a clear explanation of people groups in order that no one can pronounce missions as complete. [65]

The uncertain definition of the term "unreached" also leads to an uncertain understanding of the term "missions." Piper believes an unreached people group is reached when a local, indigenous church can evangelize its own people group.[66] However, some people groups may be closely related that a church specifically for each group is unnecessary, for example, when two unreached families share the same language. Piper states that the goal of missions includes planting churches where missionaries can properly evangelize several unreached families. This indefiniteness between missions and evangelism leads to the distinctions of E-1 (witnessing to people like oneself), E-2 (witnessing to people who speak the same language but have a different culture), and E-3 (witnessing to people who have a different language and a different culture).[67]

---

65   Ibid., 188

66   John Piper, "Missions and the End of History," <http://www.desiring-god. org/library/sermons/97/102697.html> , site editor, Desiring God Ministries, October 26, 1997, accessed on 1 March 2004; and Piper, *Let the Nations Be Glad!*, 192.

67   Piper, *Let the Nations Be Glad!*, 195 n 41, states, however, biblically, the task of missions is to reach every unreached people group.

2

CALVINISM

INTRODUCTION

To grasp Piper's appreciation for missions, his understanding of theology needs examination, for his theology lays the groundwork for his missiology. While Piper's theology is holistic, three general concepts play a significant role in much of his thought: Calvinism, and the terms, "the glory of God" and "Christian Hedonism." This chapter defines historic Calvinism and distinguishes it from Hyper-Calvinism. The chapter contrasts historic Calvinism with the Calvinism of Piper.

DEFINITION AND DESCRIPTION OF CALVINISM[1]

Calvinism is a term often used to define several ideas.[2] An overriding theme is the sovereignty of God in salvation. B. B. Warfield states that a Calvinist is a person "who casts himself on the grace of God alone, excluding every trace of dependence on self from the whole work of his salvation."[3] Charles Spurgeon goes further and equates Calvinism with the gospel:

1   Kent Ellis Sweatman, "The Doctrines of Calvinism in the Preaching of Charles Haddon Spurgeon," (Ph.D. diss., Southwestern Baptist Theological Seminary, 1998), 9–67, provides a summary of the history and doctrines of Calvinism. This section gleans from those pages.

2   Benjamin Breckinridge Warfield, *Calvin and Calvinism* (New York: Oxford University Press, 1931), 353; Sweatman, "The Doctrines of Calvinism in the Preaching of Charles Haddon Spurgeon," 9; Tom Nettles, "Missions and Creeds (Part 2)," *The Founders Journal* 18 (Fall 1994): 13–14; and Norman Geisler, *Chosen But Free*, 160.

3   Benjamin Breckinridge Warfield, *Calvin as a Theologian and Calvinism Today: Three Addresses in Commemoration of the Four-Hundredth Anniversary of the Birth of John Calvin* (Philadelphia: Presbyterian Board of

I have my own private opinion that there is no such thing as preaching Christ and   Him crucified, unless we preach what is nowadays called Calvinism. It is a nickname to call it Calvinism; Calvinism is the gospel, and nothing else. I do not believe we can preach the gospel . . . unless we preach the sovereignty of God in His dispensation of grace; nor unless we exalt the electing, unchangeable, eternal, immutable, conquering love of Jehovah; nor do I think we can preach the gospel unless we base it upon the special and particular redemption of His elect and chosen people which Christ wrought out upon the Cross; nor can I comprehend a gospel which lets saints fall away after they are called.[4]

More specifically, the theme of God's sovereignty in the soteriological elements of Calvinism is explained popularly with the acronym, "TULIP" (total depravity, unconditional election, limited atonement, irresistible grace, and perseverance of the saints).[5] While these five doctrines are not the only "points" of Calvinism,[6] they do promote the most specific and popular understanding of the term.[7] Loraine Boettner states that the Five Points of Calvinism are "pillars upon which the superstructure rests."[8] Below is a brief summary of those doctrines.

Publications, 1909), 24.

4   Charles Spurgeon, "The Early Years, 1834–1859," in *Autobiography,* rev. ed., comp. Susannah Spurgeon and Joseph Harrald, vol. 1 (Edinburgh: Banner of Truth, 1962; reprint, 1994), 168.

5   Jay Green, "Calvinism," 276; in *The Encyclopedia of Christianity,* vol. 2 (Marshallton, DE: National Foundation for Christian Education, 1968), 276. For a history of the development of Calvinism, see Sweatman, "The Doctrines of Calvinism in the Preaching of Charles Haddon Spurgeon," 14–43.

6   Edwin Palmer, *The Five Points of Calvinism* (Grand Rapids: Baker, 1980), 5, states that Calvinism has "thousands of points."

7   Sweatman, "The Doctrines of Calvinism in the Preaching of Charles Haddon Spurgeon," 13.

8   Loraine Boettner, *Doctrine of Reformed Predestination,* 8th ed. (Grand Rapids: Eerdmans, 1954), 59.

THE FIVE POINTS OF CALVINISM

Total Depravity

Total depravity, also called "total inability," states that as the result of the Fall, every person is completely unable to place faith in Christ without the aid of the Holy Spirit.[9] Whatever "good" non-Christians do is not genuinely good because non-Christians cannot do good in God's eyes.[10] While total depravity allows for social consciousness among the lost (common grace) and maintains that the non-Christians are not as evil as they can be (absolute depravity), because of original sin, there is, as Calvin states, a "hereditary corruption and depravity of our nature, extending to all the parts of the soul, which first makes us obnoxious to the wrath of God."[11]

Unconditional Election

Unconditional election states that God chooses certain individuals for salvation. This choice is based on God's own "purpose and desire," not manipulated in any way by the person.[12] Unconditional election has two parts: predestination and reprobation. Predestination is the positive form of election (God chose certain people for salvation), while reprobation is the negative form of election (God chose certain people for damnation). The Westminster Confession of Faith (1646) advocates both. It states, "By the decree of God, for the manifestation of his glory, some men and angels are predestinated unto everlasting life, and others foreordained to everlasting death."[13]

---

9   Green, "Calvinism," 275.

10   Robert L. Dabney and Jonathan Dickinson, *The Five Points of Calvinism* (Harrisonburg, VA: Sprinkle, 1992), 10.

11   Calvin, *Institutes*, 251.

12   Green, "Calvinism," 275.

13   Westminster Confession of Faith (1646), <http://www.reformed.org/documents/westminster_conf_of_faith.html#chap3>, site editor, Center for Reformed Theology and Apologetics, accessed on 22 August 2003.

Limited Atonement

Limited atonement, also called "particular redemption," states that Christ died for the elect. All those for whom he died will be saved.[14] There is debate among Calvinists regarding limited atonement. Some do not believe the term "Calvinism" (or Calvinist) should be applied to those who adhere to a position called Modified Calvinism. Modified Calvinists believe Christ's death was sufficient for all, but effective for the elect alone, also known as Amyraldianism or "4 Point Calvinism." Some Calvinists believe that Calvinism addresses only the depth (what Christ's death actually does) rather than the breadth (what Christ's death could do) of Christ's death.[15] The Synod of Dort may imply both. The Synod seems to suggest that Christ's death is sufficient for all: "The death of the Son of God is the only and most perfect sacrifice and satisfaction for sin, and is of infinite worth and value, abundantly sufficient to expiate the sins of the *whole* world."[16] The Synod also states that Christ's death was intended for the elect: "[I]t was the will of God that Christ by the blood of the cross, whereby He confirmed the new covenant, should effectually redeem out of every people, tribe, nation, and language, all those, and those only, who were from eternity chosen to salvation and given to Him by the Father."[17] The fact that Christ's death was intended only for the elect does not nullify the power of Christ's death to save the whole world. Millard Erickson infers that the difference may lie in one's understandings of the terms used in God's ordering of decrees.[18]

---

14   Green, "Calvinism," 275.
15   Sweatman, The Doctrines of Calvinism in the Preaching of Charles Haddon Spurgeon," 54.
16   Synod of Dort, <http://www.ccel.org/creeds/canons-of-dort.html>, site editor, Calvin College, accessed on 26 August 2003, italics added.
17   Ibid.
18   Millard Erickson, *Christian Theology*, 2d ed. (Grand Rapids: Baker, 1998), 931 states that this is true for Limited Atonement, too.

Two or three interpretations are offered:[19] infralapsarianism,[20] sub-lapsarianism,[21] and supralapsarianism.[22] These decrees differ as to when the decree to save humanity came, before or after the Fall. The sublapsarian position allows for Modified Calvinism.

Irresistible Grace

Irresistible grace, also called "effectual calling," states that those who respond salvifically to the call of the gospel are the elect. This call is not given to unregenerate people, though they are responsible to respond to the call.[23] Irresistible grace does not mean the elect are brought into the kingdom resisting God or the elect never oppose that grace. It means God's grace is "overwhelmingly efficacious" to overcome their resistance.[24] Martin Luther under-

---

19 For example, John Gill, *Cause of God in Truth in Four Parts with a Vindication of Part 4. From the Cavils, Calumnies, and Defamations, of Mr. Henry Heywood*, new ed. (London: W. H. Collinridge, 1855), 439, uses supralapsarianism and sublapsarianism. Boettner, *Doctrine of Reformed Predestination*, 126–30, uses infralapsarianism and supralapsarianism In Gill's and Boettner's case, the terms "infralapsarianism" and "supralapsarianism" are synonymous. Erickson, *Christian Theology*, 842–43 n 2, 931, uses all three terms. This dissertation uses Erickson's definitions.

20 Erickson, *Christian Theology*, 931. Infralaspsarianism arranges the decrees in the following order:
1. The decree to create human beings.
2. The decree to permit the fall.
3. The decree to save some and condemn others.
4. The decree to provide salvation only for the elect.

21   Ibid. Sublapsarianism arranges the decrees in the following order:
1. The decree to create human beings.
2. The decree to permit the fall.
3. The decree to provide salvation sufficient for all.
4. The decree to choose some to receive this salvation.

22   Ibid. Supralapsarianism arranges the decrees in the following order:
1. The decree to save (elect) some and reprobate others.
2. The decree to create both the elect and the reprobate.
3. The decree to permit the fall of both the elect and the reprobate.
4. The decree to provide salvation for only the elect.

23   Green, "Calvinism," 275.

24   James Montgomery Boice and Philip Graham Ryken, *The Doctrines of*

stood irresistible grace this way: "When God works in us, the will is changed under the sweet influence of the Spirit of God. Once more it desires and acts, not out of compulsion, but of its own desire and spontaneous inclination."[25]

Perseverance of the Saints

Perseverance of the saints, also called "preservation of the saints," states that God enables the elect to endure without losing salvation.[26] It does not mean that all those who profess faith in Christ are Christians. It also does not mean Christians are sinless.[27] Since salvation is a gift of God to undeserving people, perseverance of the saints means that those who have been chosen by God will not lose their salvation. Louis Berkhof explains this another way:

> His [Christ's] righteousness constitutes the perfect ground for the justification of the sinner, and it is impossible that one who is justified by the payment of such a perfect and efficacious price should again fall under condemnation. Moreover, Christ makes constant intercession for those who are given Him of the Father, and His intercessory prayer for His people is always efficacious.[28]

THE DIFFERENCE BETWEEN CALVINISM AND HYPER-CALVINISM

Although Calvinism is sometimes confused with Hyper-Calvinism,[29] they are not the same. Hyper-Calvinism combines

---

Grace (Wheaton, IL: Crossway, 2002), 135.

25 Martin Luther, *The Bondage of the Will*, trans. and ed. J. I. Packer and O. R. Johnston (Westwood, NJ: Revell, 1957), 103.

26 Green, "Calvinism," 276

27 Boettner, *The Reformed Doctrine of Predestination*, 189.

28 Louis Berkhof, *Systematic Theology*, 4th rev. and enlarged ed. (Grand Rapids: Eerdmans, 1994), 547.

29 There are many definitions of Hyper-Calvinism. For information on Hyper-Calvinism, see the following sources: Peter Toon, *The Emergence of Hyper-Calvinism in English Nonconformity, 1689–1765* (London: Olive

a denial of the free offer of the gospel with duty-faith. Calvinist theologian Iain Murray states that: "Hyper-Calvinism in its attempt to square all gospel truth with God's purpose to save the elect, denies there is a universal command to repent and believe, and asserts that we have only warrant to invite to Christ those who are conscious of a sense of sin and need."[30] The differences between the Calvinist and Hyper-Calvinist understanding of the gospel offer and duty-faith are given below.

The Gospel Offer

Calvinists affirm that Christians should offer all people the gospel, and believe that God predestined the elect.[31] Hyper-Calvinists agree with Calvinists' understanding of election, but differ with them on offering the gospel to everyone. Hyper-Calvinists

---

Tree, 1967); Thomas J. Nettles, *By His Grace and For His Glory: A Historical, Theological, and Practical Study of the Doctrine of Grace in Baptist Life* (Grand Rapids: Baker Book House, 1986); Curt D. Daniel, "Hyper-Calvinism and John Gill," (Ph.D. diss., University of Edinburgh, 1983); and Iain Murray, *The Forgotten Spurgeon* (Edinburgh: Banner of Truth, 1978); Doald MacLean, *James Durham (1622–1658): and the Gospel Offer in its Seventeenth-Century Context* (Göttingen: Vandenhoeck & Ruprecht, 2015); William VanDoodewaard, *The Marrow Controversy and the Seceder Tradition: Atonement, Saving Faith, and the Gospel Offer in Scotland (1718–1799)* (Grand Rapids: Reformation Heritage Books, 2011); and Ian J. Shaw, *High Calvinists in Action: Calvinism and the City—Manchester and London* (Oxford: Oxford University Press, 2003).

30   Murray, *The Forgotten Spurgeon*, 47. Piper affirms this definition and cites it in *Desiring God*, 237 n 14. Arminian Laurence M. Vance, *The Other Side of Calvinism* (Pensacola, FL: Vance Publications, 1999), cites this definition as well.

31   For example, The London Baptist Confession of 1644, <http://www.gty. org/~phil/creeds/bc1644.htm>, site editor, Phillip E. Johnson, accessed on 27 December 2002, states: "That Christ Jesus by his death did bring forth salvation and reconciliation only for the elect, which were those which God the Father gave him; and that *the Gospel which is to be preached to all men* as the ground of faith, is, that Jesus is the Christ, the Son of the ever blessed God, filled with the perfection of all heavenly and spiritual excellencies, and that salvation is only and alone to be had through the believing in his Name," italics added.

believe God decreed salvation to the elect alone;[32] only those who manifest signs of God's election should be offered the gospel.[33] According to the Hyper-Calvinist view, those who present the gospel to the non-elect are committing sin. Joseph Hussey, the originator of this position states, "We ought to preach the Gospel discriminately, so as in the light of the Lord to define when Christ and salvation are effectually given, where, and in whose hands, the gift lies."[34]

Duty-Faith

Calvinists affirm that God's moral law requires all men to repent and place faith in Christ.[35] Hyper-Calvinists agree, but distinguish between legal and evangelical repentance, and common and saving faith. Moral law requires legal repentance and common faith, but evangelical repentance and saving faith are God's gifts to the elect and not required by the unregenerate.[36] Hyper-Calvinists do not believe saving faith can be simultaneously a responsibility and a gift; saving faith is "a reaction caused by special [saving or irresistible] grace."[37]

---

32 Toon, *Hyper-Calvinism*, 80.

33 E. F. Chipsham, "Andrew Fuller and Fullerism: A Study in Evangelical Calvinism," *Baptist Quarterly* 20 (July 1963): 103. The manifestation of signs of "electness" is known as the "divine principle." Some signs may include confession of sin and mental distress about his soul. These people are called "sensible sinners."

34 Hussey, *God's Operations for His Grace*, 203; in Toon, *Hyper-Calvinism*, 81.

35 "The Westminister Confession of 1646," in "Center for Reformed Theology and Apologetics," <http://www.reformed.org/documents/westminster_conf_of_faith.html#chap14>, accessed on 23 January 2003, states: "Men ought not to content themselves with a general repentance, but it is every man's duty to endeavor to repent of his particular sins, particularly."

36 Toon, *Hyper-Calvinism*, 129-30.

37 Daniel, "Hyper-Calvinism and John Gill," 336.

3

PIPER'S THEOLOGY[1]

INTRODUCTION

This chapter examines Piper's understanding of Calvinism. It then explains the term "glory of God" in connection with how Piper uses it in creation, the Fall, and redemptive history. The last part of the chapter defines and explains the term "Christian Hedonism." Christian Hedonism connects with missions in the following areas: conversion, worship, love, Scripture, prayer, and suffering. The conclusion will bring together Piper's understanding of Calvinism, the glory of God, and Christian Hedonism and show that Piper falls within historic orthodox Christianity and Calvinist theology.

THE CALVINISM OF PIPER[2]

What follows is a summary of Piper's understanding of the five points of Calvinism.[3] Piper switches the "U" and the "I"

---

1   John Piper, "What We Believe About the Five Points of Calvinism," <http://desiringgod.org/library/topics/doctrines_grace/tulip.html>, site editor, Desiring God Ministries, March 1985, revised March 1998, accessed on 15 May 2000, flips the U and the I in his discussion of the TULIP because he finds people grasp the doctrine easier. In order that the reader may see the flow of Piper's belief, his format will be followed.

2   For a deeper discussion on Piper's understanding of Calvinism, see: "Calvinism," <https://www.desiringgod.org/topics/calvinism/messages>, site editor, Desiring God Ministries, accessed on 31 January 2024.

3   The Desiring God Staff, "What Does John Piper Mean When He Says That He Is a 'Seven Point' Calvinist?," <http://desiringgod.org/library/ theologicalqa/calvinism/ seven_points.html>, site editor, Desiring God Ministries, accessed on 2 September 2003, states that Piper sometimes, semi-jokingly calls himself a "seven point Calvinist." He agrees with five

in his discussion of the TULIP because he finds people grasp the doctrine easier so this format will be followed. As Piper's understanding of Calvinism lays the groundwork for his missiology and promotion of missions, understanding how Piper understands Calvinism is important.

Total Depravity

Piper understands total depravity in terms of a person's condition apart from God's grace. Piper believes each person is in complete rebellion before God and has no desire to glorify God.[4] Any type of religiosity is a form of rebellion.[5] Piper maintains that the lost sin in everything and have no ability to submit to God or do any good in any circumstance until God irresistibly calls them and causes them to see their sinfulness. He reasons since the lost are in complete rebellion, all their actions are sin because they are done apart from faith in God (Rom 14:23)[6] and therefore fail to

---

point Calvinism, but wants to emphasize two doctrines that flow from these truths: double predestination and the "best-of-all-possible-worlds." Piper's understanding of double predestination will be discussed in the section on Piper's understanding of Unconditional Election. When Piper states that this world is the "best-of-all-possible-worlds," he means that God governs history in such a manner, that in the long run, no other outcome could have better manifested his glory or provide more satisfaction for Christians; it leads to the "best-of-all-eternities."

4   John Piper, "Creation, Fall, Redemption and the Holy Spirit," http://www.desiring god.org/library/sermons/83/021284.html, site editor, Desiring God Ministries, February 12, 1984, accessed on 5 September 2003.

5   Piper, "What We Believe About the Five Points of Calvinism."

6   John Piper, "Whatever is not from Faith is Sin," <http://desiringgod.org/library/sermons/80/082480.html>, site editor, Desiring God Ministries, August 24, 1980, accessed on 18 November 2003.

glorify God,[7] even though common grace keeps them from being more evil.[8]

As a result, each person deserves eternal punishment. The reality of an eternal hell for those who do not believe demonstrates the perpetuity of sin.[9] A person's rejection of God's glory sends that person to hell, which Piper calls "an echo of the glory of God."[10] The "infinite horrors of hell" are supposed to be a reminder of the "infinite value of his [God's] glory," which each person apart from God's effectual grace has denied and rejected. Hell is the "clearest testimony to the infiniteness of the sin of failing to glorify God."[11] More on hell in the next chapters.

Irresistible Grace

If the doctrine of total depravity is true, then no person on their own can come to God. Piper's understanding of irresistible grace states that the Holy Spirit overcomes a person's rebellion and saves that person, enabling that person to cherish God's glory.[12] Piper cites the Apostle Paul's conversion as an example: Paul was a feared opponent of Christianity who was converted abruptly and without warning.[13] God saves when he desires; one does not necessarily "warm up" to the gospel.

7   John Piper, "How To Drink Orange Juice to the Glory of God," <http://www.desiringgod.org/library/topics/sin/orange_juice.html>, site editor, Desiring God Ministries, September 16, 1986, accessed on 2 September 2003.

8   Piper, "Creation, Fall, Redemption and the Holy Spirit."

9   John Piper, "Final Judgment: Eternal Life Vs Wrath and Fury," <http://www.desiringgod.org/library/sermons/80/083180.html>, site editor, Desiring God Ministries, August 31, 1980, accessed on 8 September 2003.

10   John Piper, "Behold the Kindness and the Severity of God: The Echo and Insufficiency of Hell Part Two," <http://www.desiringgod.org/library/sermons/92/062192.html>, site editor, Desiring God Ministries, June 21, 1992, accessed on 8 September 2003.

11   Piper, *Let the Nations Be Glad!*, 120–21.

12   Piper, "What We Believe About the Five Points of Calvinism."

13   John Piper, "Overflowing Grace for All Who Believe: The Conversion of the Chief of Sinners," <http://www.desiringgod.org/library/sermons/91/060991.html>, site editor, Desiring God Ministries, June 9,

Piper does believe the Holy Spirit can be resisted. A person withstands God's grace until God overcomes that person's resistance. God never forces a person to believe against that person's will. The Holy Spirit changes the will of those whom he saves by opening their eyes and causing them to see their depravity. When this occurs, a person humbly and volitionally submits to God and glorifies him by understanding that Christ is his only hope.[14]

Piper also understands that Scripture distinguishes between two calls, a general call and a specific, or an effectual, call. The general call refers to the proclamation of the gospel; it is a call meant for everyone. The specific call refers to a call that saves. The specific call is a gift. Piper comments that both calls are addressed in 1 Cor 1:23–24. The gospel is offered to all (general call), but it is heard by some in a way that saves (specific call).[15] The effectual call replaces the rebellion in a person's heart and gives new birth. God causes a person to be reborn; it was not initially by choice.[16]

Limited Atonement

The Holy Spirit irresistibly opens a person's eyes and causes them to see their depravity. Christ, by his death on the cross, takes a person's judgment upon himself, and gives the person salvation and himself glory.[17] Piper divides the atonement into two parts, the extent and nature of the atonement.

1991, accessed on 8 September 2003.

14   Piper, "What We Believe About the Five Points of Calvinism."

15   John Piper, "Called According to His Purpose," <http://www.desiring-god.org/ library/sermons/85/101385.html,> site editor, Desiring God Ministries, October 13, 1985, accessed on 8 September 2003.

16   John Piper, "God's Great Mercy and Our New Birth," <http://www. desiringgod.org/library/sermons/93/101093.html>, site editor, Desiring God Ministries, October 10, 1993, accessed on 8 September 2003.

17   Piper, "What We Believe About the Five Points of Calvinism."

The extent of the atonement

Piper believes that everyone is an "intended beneficiary" of Christ's death.[18] He also believes that Christ desires to save everyone[19] and argues that those who believe Christ died to save all are, in one sense, spiritually healthy individuals. No one can say, "I really want to be saved by believing Jesus, but I can't be because he did not die for me."[20] Piper, however, does not believe that everyone benefits from Christ's death in the same way. He explains that there is a "precious and unfathomable covenant love between Christ and his bride . . . . The death of Jesus is for the bride of Christ in a different way than it is for those who perish."[21] The difference derives from what Christ's death actually accomplished, the nature of the atonement.

The nature of the atonement

Piper states that those who maintain Christ died for everyone in the same way may have a difficult time explaining what Christ's death actually accomplished, especially for those in hell. Piper asks if Christ died for the lost the same way he did for the saved then: 1) did Christ's blood cover anyone's sins? and 2) what debt did Christ's death pay?[22] Piper is very specific with his answer to those questions. He states:

> If you say that he died for every human being in the same way, then you have to define the nature of the atonement very differently than you would if you believed that

---

18   Ibid.

19   John Piper, "Those Whom He Predestined He Also Called: Part Two,"
      <http://www. desiringgod.org/library/sermons/85/102085p.html>, site
      editor Desiring God Ministries, October 20, 1985, accessed on 8 September 2003.

20   John Piper, "For Whom Did Jesus Taste Death?," <http://www.desiring-god.org/ library/sermons/96/052696.html>, site editor, Desiring God Ministries, May 26, 1996, accessed on 8 September 2003.

21   Ibid.

22   Piper, "For Whom Did Jesus Taste Death."

Christ only died for those who actually believe. In the first case you would believe that the death of Christ did not actually save anybody; it only made all men savable. It did not actually remove God's punitive wrath from anyone, but instead created a place where people could come and find mercy—IF they could accomplish their own new birth and bring themselves to faith without the irresistible grace of God. For if Christ died for all men in the same way then he did not purchase regenerating grace for those who are saved. They must regenerate themselves and bring themselves to faith. Then and only then do they become partakers of the benefits of the cross. In other words if you believe that Christ died for all men in the same way, then the benefits of the cross cannot include the mercy by which we are brought to faith, because then all men would be brought to faith, but they aren't. But if the mercy by which we are brought to faith (irresistible grace) is not part of what Christ purchased on the cross, then we are left to save ourselves from the bondage of sin, the hardness of heart, the blindness of corruption, and the wrath of God.[23]

Unconditional Election

Since each person is dead in sin, unable to come to Christ outside of God's saving (effectual) grace, which Christ bought on the cross, salvation is completely under God's control. God elects for his purpose, and his purpose is his glory.[24] Piper states, "God's purpose is to bring about the praise of the glory of his grace. All election, all predestination, all calling, and all redemption is ac-

---

23   Piper, "What We Believe About the Five Points of Calvinism."

24   John Piper, "The Argument of Romans 9:14-16," <http://www.desiringgod.org/library/topics/doctrines_grace/romans_9.html>, site editor, Desiring God Ministries, March 1976, accessed on 19 September 2003. Also see: Piper, *The Justification of God*, 175.

cording to this purpose—for the praise of the glory of his grace."[25] In the Old Testament, God chose Israel to enjoy, praise, and proclaim his name to the peoples. In the New Testament, God chose the new Israel—the Church—to enjoy, praise, and proclaim his name to the nations.[26] Piper sees election as unconditional and individual.

Piper believes that the unconditional nature of election is why those who will be saved receive Christ. He comments that Acts 13:48 states that one's election is the reason for belief.[27] He observes that John 10:26 states that God decides who will be a Christian before birth.[28] Even something as personal as saving faith proceeds from election.[29] God elects a person apart from anything he has done, is doing, or will do.

Piper also stresses the individual nature of election as seen in predestination and reprobation.[30] When God elects for salvation, he chooses specific individuals. Commenting on 1 Cor 1: 26–31,

---

25 John Piper, "Unconditional Election And the Invincible Purpose of God," <http://www.desiringgod.org/library/sermons/02/121502.html>, site editor, Desiring God Ministries, December 15, 2002, accessed on 29 October 2003.

26 John Piper, "The Pleasure of God in Election," <http://www.desiringgod.org/ library/sermons/87/022287.html>, site editor, Desiring God Ministries, February 22, 1987, accessed on 26 September 2003. Chapter 4 will demonstrate that this was done for the glory of God.

27 Piper, "What We Believe About the Five Points of Calvinism."

28 Ibid. See also John Piper, "Jesus Is Precious Because He Gives Eternal Life," <http://www.desiringgod.org/library/sermons/82/022882.html>, site editor, Desiring God Ministries, February 28, 1982, accessed on 26 September 2003.

29 Ibid. John 8:47, 10:26, 18:37, Acts 13:28, and especially Rom 8:28–33. Piper states, "But faith is not a condition for election. Just the reverse. Election is a condition for faith. It is because God chose us before the foundation of the world that he purchases our redemption at the cross and quickens us with irresistible grace and brings us to faith."

30 John Piper, "Summary of the Sovereignty of God in Salvation: The 'Five Points' of Calvinism," <http://www.desiringgod.org/library/topics/ doctrines_grace/summary.html.>, site editor, Desiring God Ministries, December 10, 1997, accessed on 19 September 2003.

Piper states, "God does not simply elect Christ and then wait on human self-determination, to govern who will be 'in Christ.' . . . Your union with Christ is the choice and work of God."[31] When God elects for damnation, he chooses specific individuals in the same way: apart from their "willing or acting," before any good or evil deeds are done.[32]

Perseverance of the Saints

Since God saves lost people by grace through Christ's death and has elected them before time began, Christians cannot lose their salvation. However, Piper believes the doctrine of perseverance of the saints is more than "once saved, always saved." He believes God's people will persevere because God's glory is at stake. They will persevere with obedience that arises from saving faith.[33] Piper believes that justification comes at once; God makes his children persevere; and perseverance demonstrates eternal security.[34]

When God saves a person—when Christ justifies that person before God—that person is secure forever. From this point, the Christian is considered innocent before God and can never again become guilty.[35] Faith in Christ unites the Christian with God, and God enables the Christian to endure to the end.[36] The result of perseverance is obedience to God. Christians will never forsake God completely and will repent when they stumble

---

31   Piper, *The Pleasures of God*, 136.
32   The Desiring God Staff, "What Does John Piper Mean When He Says He Is a 'Seven Point' Calvinist?"
33   Piper, "What We Believe About the Five Points of Calvinism."
34   John Piper, "The Purpose and Perseverance of Faith," <http://www.desiringgod.org/library/sermons/99/101099.html>, site editor, Desiring God Ministries, October 10, 1999, accessed on 23 October 2003.
35   Ibid.
36   John Piper, "The Elect Are Kept By the Power of God," <http://www.desiringgod.org/library/sermons/93/101793.html>, site editor, Desiring God Ministries, October 17, 1993, accessed on 23 October 2003. See also: John Piper, "Sustained By the Faithfulness in God," <http://www.desiringgod.org/library/sermons/ 88/011788.html>, site editor, Desiring God Ministries, January 17, 1988, accessed on 29 October 2003.

and fall into sin. There is no continual lapsed state.[37] Christians
will guard against temptations and are supposed to be concerned
about their individual salvation.[38] Piper states God justifies in this
way to minimize boasting, to proclaim God's glory, and to secure
eternally salvation.[39]

PIPER'S DEFINITION AND EXPLANATION OF THE GLORY OF GOD[40]

Piper's understanding of the term "glory of God" governs his
understanding of Calvinism. Piper does not specifically define the
word "glory," by itself; instead he summarizes Edwards' understanding of the term. Edwards, according to Piper, explains that
glory: 1) signifies what is internal, 2) conveys exhibition or emana-
tion, 3) indicates understanding excellence, or 4) suggests praise.[41]
Piper applies Edwards' understanding to his own definition of
the "glory of God," contrasts it with God's holiness (being God's
"incomparable perfection and greatness of his divine nature"[42])
and defines the glory of God as the "moral beauty of God's manifold perfections . . . his infinite, eternal, and unchangeable being,
and his wisdom, power, holiness, justice, goodness, and truth."[43]

---

37 Piper, "What We Believe About the Five Points of Calvinism."
38 John Piper, "Eternal Security Is a Community Project," <http://www.
    desiringgod.org/library/sermons/96/081896.html>, site editor, Desiring
    God Ministries, August 18, 1996, accessed on 23 October 2003.
39 Piper, "The Purpose and Perseverance of Faith."
40 For a detailed look into Piper's understanding of the glory of God see:
    "Glory of God," <https://www.desiringgod.org/topics/the-glory-of-god/
    messages>, site editor, Desiring God Ministries, 31 January 2024.
41 Edwards, *The End for Which God Created the World*, 230–37.
42 John Piper, "To Him Be Glory Forevermore, <http://www.desiringgod.
    org/ResourceLibrary/Sermons/ByTopic/3/1914_To_Him_ Be_Glo-
    ry_Forevermore/>, site editor, Desiring God Ministries, December 17,
    2006, accessed on 5 February 2010.
43 John Piper, "A Response to Richard Mouw's Treatment of Christian
    Hedonism in *The God Who Commands*," <http://www.desiringgod.org/
    library/topics/christian_hedonism/ mouw.html>, site editor, Desiring
    God Ministries, accessed on 8 January 2004. See also *The Justification of*

Piper argues that no text in Scripture shows God's passion for his own glory more than Isa 48:9-11, which states: "For my name's sake I defer my anger, for the sake of my praise I restrain it for you, that I may not cut you off. Behold, I have refined you, but not as silver; I have tried you in the furnace of affliction. For my own sake, for my own sake, I do it, for how should my name be profaned? My glory I will not give to another ... [This text] hammers home to us the centrality of God in his own affections."[44]

CHRISTIAN HEDONISM[45]

Piper's understanding of God's glory plays a prominent role in his understanding of the Christian life. Piper believes that Christians need to pursue God's glory, and in doing this they will pursue their ultimate joy. The pursuit of God's glory as Christian Hedonism. Living like a "Christian Hedonist" will impact the lives of Christians regarding missions. The way a Christian lives impacts how the gospel message is shared and received at home and abroad.

Definition and Foundation of Christian Hedonism

The foundation of Christian Hedonism is God's happiness.[46] God is infinitely happy with himself, loves nothing more than himself,[47] and is completely satisfied with the love he has for

---

God, 121; and *Desiring God*, 41–43, 308.

44   John Piper, "Biblical Texts to Show God's Zeal for His Own Glory," <http://www.desiringgod.org/ResourceLibrary/Articles/By-Date/2007/2510_Biblical_Texts_to_Show_Gods_Zeal_for_His_Own_Glory/>, site editor, Desiring God Ministries, 24 November 2007, accessed on 5 February 2010. Italics his.

45   For a more detailed look at Christian Hedonism and how Piper views it, see: "Christian Hedonism," <https://www.desiringgod.org/topics/christian-hedonism/messages>, site editor, Desiring God Ministries, 31 January 2024.

46   Piper, *Desiring God*, 33.

47   John Piper, "The Happiness of God," <http://www.desiringgod.org/

himself.[48] God is happy because all his decisions are righteous and cannot be frustrated. God is sovereign over all his decisions; they are made "out of love to his own glory."[49] God works "all things after the counsel of his will" (Eph 1:11), from minor events to life threatening happenings to the crucifixion of Christ. Based on this foundation, Christian Hedonism is built on five premises:

1) The desire to be happy is universal and not sinful.
2) People should never resist the desire to be happy and should satisfy this longing with what will provide the greatest gratification.
3) The most satisfying happiness is in God.
4) Happiness in God reaches its peak when it is shared with others.
5) "The chief end of man is to glorify God BY enjoying him forever."[50]

Christian Hedonism in Relation to Conversion

Conversion is a miracle given by God to his elect that enables them to repent and place their faith in Christ.[51] Conversion occurs only after regeneration; God must overcome a person's resistance and enable that person to see their own sin and need for Christ. Piper states that at conversion, the person will chase joy in the

---

library/ sermons/83/091183.html>, site editor, Desiring God Ministries, September 11, 1983, accessed on 18 December 2003.

48 John Piper, "The Pleasure of God in His Creation," <http://www.desiringgod.org/library/sermons/87/020887.html>, site editor, Desiring God Ministries, February 8, 1987, accessed on 18 December 2003.

49 Piper, "The Happiness of God."

50 John Piper, "Why I Did Not Say, 'God Did Not Cause the Calamity, but He Can Use it for Good,'" <http://www.desiringgod.org/library/fresh_words/2001/ 091701.html>, site editor, Desiring God Ministries, September 17, 2001, accessed on 3 December 2003.

51 Piper, *Desiring God*, 61–62.

glory of God and strive for God's glory in the same manner as God pursues the glory of himself.[52]

Piper gives six reasons that outline the connection between conversion and the glory of God. First, everything begins with God. God created humans to glorify God (Isa 43:6–7). Second, a person's duty is to glorify God in everything he does (1 Cor 10:31). The way the person glorifies God is joyfully to cherish him above all things and to proclaim God's glory to the whole world. Everyone has this responsibility, including those who have never heard the gospel. Third, a person fails to glorify God (Rom 1:23, 3:23) because the person exchanges God's glory for something of lesser value. This is sin. Everyone has chosen to be sinful. Fourth, a person is damned (Rom 6:23, 2 Thes 1:9) because the person holds God's glory in contempt. Sin is an infinite offense to God, and, therefore must be infinitely punished. Fifth, Christ came to save people from hell by dying in their place and rising from the dead (1 Tim 1:15, Rom 4:25). In the death and resurrection of Christ, God protects the value of his glory by giving people a chance to repent, place their faith in him, and glorify God. Christ satisfied God's wrath and justifies a person by taking his sin. Sixth, the benefits of Christ's death are applied only to those who place their faith in him (Acts 3:19, 16:31). The condition that must be met is conversion.[53]

Christian Hedonism in Relation to Worship

One day, people from all people groups will worship God. Worship is not optional—it is a person's most important responsibility. Worship is honoring the glory of God,[54] being fulfilled in him, and treasuring him above all things. Practically, worship

---

52   Piper, "A Response to Richard Mouw's Treatment of Christian Hedonism," in *The God Who Commands*.

53   Ibid., 55–61.

54   John Piper, "Worship Is an End in Itself," <http://desiringgod.org/library/ sermons/81/091381.html>, site editor, Desiring God Ministries, September 13, 1981, accessed on 9 January 2004.

consists of internal, daily expressions of joyful loyalty to God.[55] Worship combines the intellect and the emotion. It occurs only when a Christian has solid, biblical, intellectual conceptions of God's glory. Worship, while not emotionalism, is fake unless it includes the emotions.[56] Worship expresses sorrow for sin, longing, thankfulness, and hope in God.[57]

Worship must be God-centered and is an end in itself.[58] There are three stages to worship: the start of worship, a longing to be free and happy in worship, and "unencumbered joy" in worship. The first stage is the lowest stage. It is where a Christian returns during challenging times in life. It is characterized by emptiness that barely senses any desire to worship. Here, God provides the Christian grace to repent for the lack of desire. The second stage is where the Christian desires to taste true worship. The heart is not as enthusiastic as necessary, but it remembers the grace of God. The last stage is where the Christian is happy and gratified with the glory of God. The person is able, without constraint, to feel joy in the manifold perfections of God.[59] In order to arrive at the final stage, Piper suggests the following: praying for an open heart; meditating on Scripture; foregoing worldly distractions; trusting in truth that is already received; resting and being alert for worship services; not complaining; having a teachable spirit; focusing attention on love for God; thinking about what is sung, prayed, and preached; and desiring truth found in Scripture.[60]

---

55   John Piper, "The Inner Essence of Worship," <http://desiringgod.org/ library/ sermons/97/111697.html>, site editor, Desiring God Ministries, November 16, 1997, accessed on 9 January 2004.

56   Piper, "Worship Is an End in Itself," and Piper, *Desiring God*, 81.

57   Piper, "Worship Is an End in Itself."

58   John Piper, "The Inner Essence of Worship," <http://desiringgod.org/ library/ sermons/97/111697.html>, site editor, Desiring God Ministries, November 16, 1997, accessed on 16 January 2004.

59   Piper, *Desiring God*, 85–86.

60   John Piper, "Take Heed How You Hear!," <http://desiringgod.org/ library/fresh_ words/1998/030198.html>, site editor, Desiring God Ministries, March 1, 1998, accessed on 16 January 2004.

Christian Hedonism in Relation to Love

Piper believes love only occurs when a Christian is motivated to pursue his greatest pleasure, the glory of God.[61] Love is not just doing right or denying oneself to benefit another.[62] Love must include the emotions.[63] Love is an "overflow of joy in God that gladly meets the needs of others."[64] Love is also an act of God's grace. Those who experience his grace will overflow with joy; their joy will overflow in generosity to others and initiate an intense desire to help those in need.[65]

Christian Hedonism in Relation to Scripture

The Bible, along with general revelation, are means by which God manifests his glory. Piper reasons that the Word of God provides the means for the Christian's joy. God gave saving faith as a gift to the elect. From saving faith arises joy, and from joy arises hope in the Word of God.[66] Piper believes one of the best ways to glorify God by enjoying him is through Scripture meditation.[67] As a main objective of Satan is to destroy the Christian's joy, if a Christian does not know Scripture, he cannot savor it, and he cannot use it during times of spiritual warfare.[68] Piper connects Scripture meditation with prayer. He states that meditation on Scripture helps guide prayers and builds faith. The Bible changes

---

61   Piper, *Desiring God*, 119, original italics.

62   Ibid., 120.

63   "It Is Often Said That Love Is an Act of the Will, Not an Emotion. What Is Your View?," <http://www.desiringgod.org/library/theological_qa/chr_hedonism/love.html>, site editor, Desiring God Ministries, accessed on 2 March 2004.

64   John Piper, "Love," <http://www.desiringgod.org/library/sermons/83/100283.html>, site editor, Desiring God Ministries, October 2, 1983, accessed on 2 March 2004.

65   Piper, *Desiring God*, 118–19.

66   Ibid.

67   John Piper, "Thy Word I Have Treasured in My Heart," <http://desiringgod.org/library/sermons/97/010597.html>, site editor, Desiring God Ministries, January 5, 1997, accessed on 15 January 2004.

68   Piper, *Desiring God*, 143–57.

the Christian morally and spiritually, and prayer becomes more God centered.[69] The Word of God opens the power of the gospel and enables the Christian to see more of the glory of God.[70]

Christian Hedonism in Relation to Prayer

Along with Scripture, prayer is the "parallel rail" that empowers the Christian to persevere.[71] Prayer is the heart of Christian Hedonism; it unites the glory of God and the Christian's joy. Prayer glorifies God because it shows a person's dependence on him. Prayer provides joy to the Christian because God gives the Christian mercy and grace to fellowship with God. In prayer, the Christian is able to express his inner longings for Christ and his desire to love others for the glory of God.[72] Prayer fulfills God's ultimate goal "to uphold and display his glory for the enjoyment of all the redeemed from all the nations."[73]

Since God is glorified and the Christian receives joy in prayer, Piper explains that the Christian is supposed to pray to God about everything. Often, however, prayer is used incorrectly. Prayer is like a "walkie-talkie" used in wartime. Its purpose is for the mission of bearing fruit. Many Christians, however, do not believe they are in war.[74] Christians fail to pray according to God's will (1 John 5:14), have unrepentant sin (Ps 66:18), focus on man centered motives (Jas 4:3), do not believe that God will answer their prayer (Mark 11:24), fail to notice the testing of God (Luke18:1), and fail to see that God is answering their prayer (Dan 10:2,

---

69 John Piper, "A Summary Theology of Prayer" <http://desiringgod.org/ library/fresh_words/2002/062602.html>, site editor, Desiring God Ministries, June 26, 2002, accessed on 16 January 2004.

70 John Piper, "Prayer: The Work of Missions," <http://desiringgod.org/ library/ topics/prayer/prayer_missions.html>, site editor, Desiring God Ministries, October 30, 1983, accessed on 16 January 2004.

71 John Piper, "O Lord, Open My Eyes!," <http://desiringgod.org/library/ sermons/98/010498.html>, site editor, Desiring God Ministries, January 4, 1998, accessed on 14 January 2004.

72 Piper, *Desiring God*, 160–74.

73 Piper, *Let the Nations Be Glad!*, 63.

74 Ibid., 47–62.

12).[75] They have tried to turn the "walkie-talkie" into a "domestic intercom."[76] Piper encourages Christians to rethink their attitude toward prayer, make a specific time and place for it, and pray using Scripture as a guide.[77]

Christian Hedonism in Relation to Suffering

In sickness and persecution, the Christian glorifies God by demonstrating that God is the foundation for his joy, not health, prosperity, or earthly or material pleasures.[78] This belief is especially helpful as Piper reminds the Christian the cost of glorifying God is great:

> More and more I am persuaded from Scripture and from the history of missions that God's design for the evangelization of the world and the consummation of his purposes includes the suffering of his ministers and missionaries. To put it more plainly and specifically, God designs that the suffering of his ambassadors is one essential means in the triumphant spread of the Good News among all the peoples of the world.[79]

Piper centers his belief in suffering on the resurrection. If the resurrection were not true, the Christian is a fool and should live an ordinary life, not worrying about eternity.[80] Since the resurrection is true, suffering is God's gift (Phil 1:29), and no Christian

---

75   John Piper, "Praying from the Fullness of the Word," <http://desiring-god.org/ library/sermons/96/122996.html>, site editor, Desiring God Ministries, December 29, 1996, accessed on 19 January 2004.

76   Piper, *Let the Nations Be Glad!*, 47–48

77   Piper, *Desiring God*, 183.

78   Piper, *Desiring God*, 261, 288. Piper does not separate sickness and persecution in suffering because he believes the line that divides them can be unclear. See Ibid., 256, 259–61.

79   John Piper, *Filling up the Afflictions of Christ: The Cost of Bringing the Gospel to the Nations in the Lives of William Tyndale, Adoniram Judson, and John Paton* (Wheaton, IL: Crossway, 2009), 14.

80   Ibid., 260.

is "without cross-bearing and daily dying."[81] When a Christian rejoices in the midst of suffering, he glorifies God's sovereignty. Suffering is not an accident, nor is it senseless. God will not turn away from the Christian.[82] In the light of eternity, sufferings are brief and help refine and enable the Christian to glorify God in a deeper manner.[83] At the second coming, suffering will be gone, and joy in God's glory will be multiplied beyond comparison.[84]

Piper realizes that Satan tries to use sickness and persecution to destroy the Christian's faith. He also knows that God sovereignly governs the actions of Satan, who may only accomplish what God permits. To help the Christian believe that all things work together for good,[85] Piper provides several reasons why suffering aids the Christian. Suffering helps the Christian morally and spiritually by increasing holiness and hope in the resurrection.[86] Romans 5:1–8 explains that suffering is part of God's plan to produce perseverance for his name. Perseverance produces stronger faith in Christ and intensifies hope in the resurrection. Suffering aids the Christian's intimacy with God by enabling him to have a greater understanding of Christ. Philippians 3:1–8 states that suffering helps the Christian count all earthly treasures as loss for Christ.[87] Suffering helps the Christian in missions by allowing

---

81 Ibid., 263–64.
82 John Piper, "Sustained By Sovereign Grace–Forever," <http://desiringgod. org/ library/sermons/96/061696.html>, site editor, Desiring God Ministries, June 16, 1996, accessed on 26 January 2004.
83 Piper, "Joy Through the Fiery Test of Faith."
84 John Piper, "Why We Can Rejoice in Suffering," <http://desiringgod.org/ library/sermons/94/102394.html>, site editor, Desiring God Ministries, October 23, 1994, accessed on 26 January 2004.
85 John Piper, "Ruth: Sweet and Bitter Providence," <http://desiringgod. org/library/sermons/84/070784.html>, site editor, Desiring God Ministries, July 1, 1984, accessed on 23 January 2004.
86 John Piper, "Called to Rejoice in Suffering: For Holiness and Hope," <http://desiringgod.org/library/sermons/92/081692.html>, site editor, Desiring God Ministries, August 16, 1992, accessed on 23 January 2004.
87 John Piper, "Called to Rejoice in Suffering: That We Might Gain Christ,"

him to demonstrate Christ's worth. Colossians 1:24–29 states that
Paul "filled up" what was "lacking" in Christ's afflictions. What
Christ's afflictions lack is an evangelistic witness in all the nations;[88] Piper believes the Great Commission will not be completed without martyrdom.[89] Suffering helps the Christian treasure
God by demonstrating that the temporal nature of pain increases
the Christian's desire for glory. In 2 Cor 4:16–18 Paul states that
his afflictions are light compared to his future glory.[90]

God is in control of all things, including the worst evil. God
uses evil for his glory. Piper quotes Edwards at length regarding
the demonstration of God's glory in his sovereignty and happiness
over evil. He states:

> It is a proper and excellent thing for infinite glory to
> shine forth; and for the same reason, it is proper that the
> shining forth of God's glory should be complete; that is,
> that all parts of his glory should shine forth, that every
> beauty should be proportionally effugent, that the be-
> holder may have a proper notion of God. It is not prop-
> er that one glory should be exceedingly manifested, and
> another not at all. . . .
>
> So evil is necessary, in order to the highest happiness of
> the creature, and the completeness of that communica-
> tion of God, for which he made the world; because the

<http://desiringgod.org/library/sermons/92/082392.html>, site editor,
Desiring God Ministries, August 23, 1992, accessed on 26 January
2004.

88   John Piper, "Called to Rejoice in Suffering: To Finish the Aim of Christ's
     Afflictions," <http://desiringgod.org/library/sermons/92/083092.html>,
     site editor, Desiring God Ministries, August 30, 1992, accessed on 26
     January 2004.

89   John Piper, "Arming Yourself with the Purpose to Suffer," <http://desir-
     inggod.org/library/sermons/94/100294.html>, site editor, Desiring God
     Ministries, October 2, 1994, accessed on 26 January 2004

90   John Piper, "Called to Rejoice in Suffering: For an Eternal Weight of
     Glory," <http://desiringgod.org/library/sermons/92/090692.html>, site
     editor, Desiring God Ministries, September 6, 1992, accessed on 26
     January 2004.

creature's happiness consists in the knowledge of God, and the sense of his love. And if the knowledge of him be imperfect, the happiness of the creature must be proportionally imperfect.[91]

THE CONNECTION BETWEEN PIPER'S CALVINISM, HIS UNDERSTANDING OF THE GLORY OF GOD, AND CHRISTIAN HEDONISM

The components of Piper's theology unite around the theme of the glory of God. This theme is prevalent in his understanding of Calvinism and widespread in his understanding of Christian Hedonism. He incorporates the glory of God into each of the five points of Calvinism. Unregenerate man is dead and unable to see God's glory (total depravity). God elects some for salvation and some for damnation for his glory (unconditional election). The benefits of Christ's death are applied to the elect alone to demonstrate God's glory (limited atonement). A person is not able to cherish God's glory until God overcomes his resistance (irresistible grace). God enables the elect to persevere because God's glory is at stake (perseverance of the saints).[92]

---

91 Jonathan Edwards in John Piper, "Is God Less Glorious Because He Ordained that Evil Be," <http://www.desiringgod.org/library/topics/suffering/god_ and_evil. html>, site editor, Desiring God Ministries, July 1988, accessed on 3 December 2003.

92 For example, Piper, "What We Believe About the Five Points of Calvinism." Some other works by Piper connect his understanding of Calvinism to God's glory. Some of them are: John Piper, "How To Drink Orange Juice to the Glory of God;" John Piper, "Those Whom He Predestined He Also Called: Part One," <http://www.desiring god.org/library/sermons/85/102085.html>, site editor, Desiring God Ministries, October 20, 1985, accessed on 9 February 2004; John Piper, "Those Whom He Predestined He Also Called: Part Two;" Ibid., "For Whom Did Jesus Taste Death?;" John Piper, "The Argument of Romans 9:14-16;" Ibid., "Those Whom He Foreknew He Predestined," <http://www. desiringgod.org/library/sermons/85/ 101385p.html>, site editor, Desiring God Ministries, October 13, 1985, accessed on 9 February 2004; John Piper, "The Purpose and Perseverance of Faith;" and John Piper,

Piper also connects the glory of God with Christian Hedonism. Christian Hedonism's definition states that the purpose of
humankind is "to glorify God BY enjoying Him forever."[93] Ideas
of Christian Hedonism that explain the interaction between God's
glory and humanity's joy include: Piper's understanding of conversion, worship, love, Scripture, prayer, and suffering.[94] Piper, as
well, connects Calvinism and Christian Hedonism with the glory
of God. He links them together in proposed titles for a sermon
on Augustine.[95] He directly connects them when he states that

---

"The Doctrine of Perseverance," <http://www.desiringgod.org/library/
topics/racial_harmony/sovereignty_soul_ dynamic.html>, site editor,
Desiring God Ministries, April 24, 1988, accessed on 9 February 2004.

93   Piper, *Desiring God*, 17.

94   Aside from the works already cited in this chapter, some other works
that connect Christian Hedonism to glory of God include: John Piper, "Conversion to Christ," <http://www. desiringgod.org/library/ser-
mons/83/091883.html>, site editor, Desiring God Ministries, September
18, 1983, accessed on 10 February 2004; John Piper, "Worship God!,"
<http://desiring god.org/library/sermons/ 91/091591.html>, site editor,
Desiring God Ministries, September 15, 1991, accessed on 10 February
2004; John Piper, "Worship is an End Itself," <http://desiringgod.org/
library/sermons/81/ 091381.htmll>, site editor, Desiring God Ministries,
September 13, 1981, accessed on 10 February 2004; John Piper, "Prayer,"
<http://desiringgod.org/library/sermons/83/102383.html>, site editor,
Desiring God Ministries, October 23, 1983, accessed on 10 February
2004; John Piper, "Toward the Tithe and Beyond," <http://www.desir-
inggod.org/library/sermons/95/091095.html>, site editor, Desiring God
Ministries, September 10, 1995, accessed on 10 February 2004; John
Piper, "Let Marriage Be Held in Honor Among All," <http://www.desir-
inggod.org/library/sermons/91/ 081191.html>, site editor, Desiring God
Ministries, August 11, 1991, accessed on 10 February 2004; and John
Piper, "By What Death Will You Glorify God?," <http://www.desiring-
god.org/ library/fresh_ words/1999/090199.html>, site editor, Desiring
God Ministries, August 11, 1991, accessed on 10 February 2004.

95   John Piper, "The Swan is Not Silent," <http://www.desiringgod.org/
library/ biographies/98augustine.html>, site editor, Desiring God
Ministries, 1998, accessed on 10 February 2004. The other two titles
he thought about using were: "The Place of Pleasure in the Exposition
and Defense of Evangelical Calvinism" or "The Augustinian Roots of
Christian Hedonism.

he sees Calvinism "with its massive vision of the glory of God—through the lens of Christian Hedonism."[96]

---

96 John Piper, "The Sovereignty of God and the Soul Dynamic," <http:// www.desiringgod.org/library/topics/racial_harmony/sovereignty_soul_ dynamic.html>, site editor, Desiring God Ministries, February 4, 2002, accessed on 9 February 2004.

4

CALVINIST MISSIOLOGY[1]

CALVINISTS MISSIONS BEFORE THE PROTESTANT MODERN MISSIONS MOVEMENT

Missions did not stop with the apostles and then restart with William Carey. The Church of the East in greater Iran was active in missionary efforts. Protestants did not geographically expand as Catholics during the Reformation; nonetheless, the widely held belief that Protestants were not interested in the unreached or "non-Christian peoples" is only partially true.[2] Calvinists were some of the most influential missionaries of this period. Before the Protestant Modern Missions Movement, when Protestant and Calvinist missions greatly expanded, people such as John Calvin sent his followers to Brazil to, among other things, evangelize the locals.[3] Jean de Léry, a person who went to Brazil on the mission,

---

1   The first paragraph in this section gleans from Philip O. Hopkins, "Mission to Unreached People Groups," in *The Mission of God*, ed. Bruce Ashford (Nashville: Broadman and Holman, 2011), 175-85.

2   Kenneth S. Latourette, *A History of the Expansion of Christianity*, vol. 3, *Three Centuries of Advance, A.D. 1500-A.D. 1800* (New York: Cambridge University Press, 1939), 25-26; in Donald Dean Smeeton, "William Tyndale's Suggestions for a Protestant Missiology," *Missiology: An International Review* 14, no. 2 (April 1986), 174, gives several reasons for the lack of involvement in missions among Protestants during the Reformation period: 1) a focus on developing their own theology; 2) denial of the requirement to share Christ; 3) involvement in religious wars; 4) lack of political encouragement among Protestant governments; 5) lack of an official clergy; and 6) little contact with unreached peoples. See also: Stephen Neill, *A History of Christian Missions*, rev. (London: Penguin, 1990), 187-204.

3   Amy Glassner Gordon, "The First Protestant Missionary Effort: Why Did It Fail?," *International Bulletin for Missionary Research* 8, no. 1 (Jan

seemed excited about the potential of many unreached people hearing the gospel for the first time when he reportedly said, "the church of Geneva at once gave thanks to God for the extension of the reign of Jesus Christ in a country so distant and likewise so foreign and among a nation entirely without the knowledge of the true God."[4] One reason the Puritans (theologically Calvinist) came to New England was to evangelize the Native Americans.[5] John Eliot's ministry among the Indians of Massachusetts is another example of a Calvinist evangelizing cross-culturally. Eliot helped in the translation of the Bible into the language of the Native Americans, trained local Christian leaders in doctrine, and encouraged the American Indian believers to assume responsibility and authority for their fellowships.[6]

Calvinists David Brainerd and Jonathan Edwards were helpful in creating a missions mindset during this time. Brainerd's missiological methods should not be emulated, but he, like Eliot, became a missionary to the American Indians (as did Jonathan Edwards). Brainerd's diaries, published by Edwards, served to motivate many who went to the unreached, including Carey (1761-1834); Thomas Coke (1747-1814), founder of Methodist missions; and Henry Martyn (1781-1812), Anglican missionary to India and Iran.[7] Timothy George states that Carey had much

---

1984) 12-14.

4   Jean de Léry, Journal de Bord de Jean de Léry en la Terre de Brésil 1557, présénté et commenté par M.R. Mayeux (Paris, 1957), quoted in R. Pierce Beaver, "The Genevan Mission to Brazil," in The Heritage of John Calvin (ed. John Bratt; Grand Rapids: Eerdmans, 1973), 61, quoted in Kenneth J. Stewart, "Calvinism and Missions: The Contested Relationship Revisited," Themelios 34, no. 1 (April 2009), <http://www.thegos-pelcoalition.org/publications/34-1/calvinismandmissionsthecontestedre-lationshiprevisited/#a29>, site editor, Themelios, April 2009, accessed on 22 January 2010.

5   John B. Carpenter, "New England Puritans: Grandparents of Modern Protestant Missions," Missiology: An International Review XXX, no. 4 (Oct 2002), 519.

6   Stewart, "Calvinism and Missions."

7   Ibid., 526-27.

of it memorized.[8] George also quotes Martyn's admiration of the diary:

> Read David Brainerd today and yesterday, and find as usual my spirit greatly benefited by it. I long to be like him; let me forget the world and be swallowed up in a desire to glorify God. Read Brainerd. I feel my heart knit to this dear man, and really rejoice to think of meeting him in heaven.[9]

The impact Brainerd and Edwards had on the Modern Missions Movement should not be underestimated. Writer J.A. De-Jong states, "If the two major forces behind the nineteenth-century Anglo-American missions could be isolated, a convincing case could be constructed for their being the [Calvinist] theology of Jonathan Edwards and the example of David Brainerd."[10]

CALVINIST MISSIONS DURING THE PROTESTANT MODERN MISSIONS MOVEMENT

The Protestant Modern Missions Movement is traditionally said to have begun with Carey. Church growth expert Ralph Winter proposed that the time frame of this movement be divided into three eras with two transition periods: Era One: Coastlands, 1792-1910; Transition One: 1865-1910; Era Two: Inland, 1865-1980; Transition Two: 1934-1980; and Era Three: Hidden Peoples 1980-Present.[11] In each of these eras, some of the most influential

---

8   Timothy George, "The Evangelical Revival and the Missionary Awakening," in *The Great Commission: Evangelicals and the History of World Missions*, ed. Martin Klauber and Scott Manetsch (Nashville: Broadman & Holman, 2008), 47.

9   Constance E. Padwick, *Henry Martyn: Confessor of the Faith* (London: InterVarsity,1953), 49; in George, "The Evangelical Revival and the Missionary Awakening," 47.

10   J.A. DeJong, *As the Waters Cover the Sea: Millennial Expectations in the Rise of Anglo-American Missions, 1640-1810* (Kampen, the Netherlands: J.H. Kok N.V., 1970); in Carpenter, "New England Puritans," 526.

11   Ralph Winter, "The Concept of a Third Era in Missions," *EMQ* 17, no.

missionaries affirmed Calvinist (or at least Calvinistic) theology. While it is not within the scope of this chapter to describe all the Calvinist missionaries of each period, a sampling are worth mentioning to show that Calvinists were involved in each period.

Era 1

Of the many Calvinists during this period, three of the better known ones were William Carey, Andrew Fuller, and Adoniram Judson. George calls Carey an "evangelical Calvinist."[12] Tom Ascol, head of Founders Ministries, an organization that seeks to remind Southern Baptists of their Calvinist roots, quotes a section in the Serampore Compact – a document that Carey and other missionaries drafted – which addresses their belief of God's sovereignty in salvation:

> We are firmly persuaded that Paul might plant and Apollos water, in vain, in any part of the world, did not God give the increase. We are sure that only those ordained to eternal life will believe, and that God alone can add to the church such as shall be saved. Nevertheless we cannot but observe with admiration that Paul, the great champion for the glorious doctrine of free and sovereign grace, was the most conspicuous for his personal zeal in the word of persuading men to be reconciled to God. In this respect he is a noble example for our imitation.[13]

---

    2 (April 1981), 72. See also: Ralph Winter, "3 Men, 3 Eras: The Flow of Missions," *Mission Frontiers* 3, no. 2 (Feb 1981), 1, 4-7; and Ralph Winter, "Four Men, Three Eras," *Mission Frontiers* 19 (Nov 1997), 11-12, 18.

12   Timothy George, *Faithful Witness, the Life and Witness of William Carey* (Birmingham, AL: New Hope, 1991), 57.

13   Serampore Compact, quoted in Tom Ascol, "Calvinism, Evangelism & Founders Ministries," *Founders Journal* (Summer 2001), 1-21; <http://www.founders.org/journal/ fj45/editorial.html#N_40_>, site editor, Founders Ministries, accessed on 22 January 2010. In footnote 40, Ascol provides information as to where the Serampore Covenant can be obtained.

Fuller (1754-1815), while not a missionary, was a Calvinist pastor. He was a contemporary of Carey and traveled to garner support for Carey. Baptist historian Thomas J. Nettles states that Fuller both promoted missions and Calvinism.[14] Piper also calls Fuller a "Calvinist" and asserts that he was "the" main promoter of the Baptist Missionary Society for twenty-one years.[15] In Fuller's work, *Gospel Worthy of all Acceptation; or, The Duty of Sinners to Believe in Jesus Christ*, he explains that the lost are commanded to place their faith in Christ:

> *From What has been advanced, we may form a judgment of our duty, as ministers of the word, in dealing with the unconverted.* The work of the Christian ministry, it has been said, is to *preach the Gospel*, or to hold up the free grace of God through Jesus Christ, as the only way of a sinner's salvation. This is, doubt-less, true; and if this be no the leading theme of our ministries, we had better be any thing than preachers. *Woe unto us, if we preach not the Gospel!*[16]

Judson (1788–1850), a missionary to Burma, is another example of a cross-cultural worker whose Calvinism coexists with

---

14 Thomas J. Nettles, *By His Grace and For His Glory: A Historical, Theological, and Practical Study of the Doctrines of Grace in Baptist Life* (Grand Rapids: Baker Book House, 1986), 129.

15 John Piper, "Holy Faith, Worthy Gospel, World Vision: Andrew Fuller's Broadsides Against Sandemanianism, Hyper-Calvinism, and Global Unbelief," <http://www.desiringgod.org/ResourceLibrary/ConferenceMessages/ByConference/13/1977_Holy_Faith_Worthy_Gospel_World_Vision/>, site editor, Desiring God Ministries, February 6, 2007 accessed on 5 February 2010.

16 Andrew Fuller, *Gospel Worthy of all Acceptation; or, The Duty of Sinners to Believe in Jesus Christ* (Boston: American Doctrinal Tract Society, 1846), 89; in Google Books, <http://books.google.com/books?id=D-mYAAAAYAAJ&printsec=frontcover&dq=The+Gospel+Worthy+of+All+Acceptation&ei=7tZS5ywBZuQywTRzsSnBA&cd =1#v=onepage&q=&f=false>, site editor, Google Books, accessed on 22 January 2010, italics his.

his heart for the lost. In a sermon, he intertwines his understanding of election and the proclamation of the gospel:

> The true shepherd calleth his own sheep by name, and the sheep hear his voice; and when he putteth them forth, he goeth before them, and the sheep follow him, for they know his voice. Christ calls his people by his word; he points out the true and living way; and he has gone before his people in that way, setting them an example which they may safely follow. We come now to consider the main duty of a Christian pastor. First he must call his people. Though enclosed in the Saviour's electing love, they may still be wandering on the dark mountains of sin, and he must go after them; perhaps he must seek them in very remote regions, in the very outskirts of the wilderness of heathenism. And as he cannot at first distinguish them from the rest, who will never listen and be saved, he must lift up his voice to all, without discrimination, and utter, in the hearing of all, that invitation of mercy and love which will penetrate the ears and the hearts of the elect only. And when they listen, he must show them the way – Christ, the way, the truth, and the life; teaching them to observe all things which he has commanded."[17]

Era 2[18]

In Era 2, John G. Paton, Samuel Zwemer, and Johannes Verkuyl, will be given as examples of Calvinist missionary zeal.

---

17   Francis Wayland, ed. *Memoir of the Life and Labor of the Rev. Adoniram Judson, D.D.*, 2 vols. (Boston: Phillips, Sampson, & Co., 1835), 2:490.

18   There are other notable Calvinists with a heart for missions of this period. A.T. Pierson (1837-1911), an American Presbyterian pastor, was instrumental in the Student Volunteer Missions Movement. John L. Nevius (1829-1893), known for developing the "Nevius Plan," an idea that supported the notion of self-supporting and self-governing churches, could also be described as holding to Calvinist theology. Johanna Veenstra (1894-1993) was instrumental in the Christian Reformed

Paton (1824-1907), a Scottish missionary in the New Hebrides in the southern Pacific, lost his wife and child to sickness on the field less than a year after arriving.[19] He called himself a "strong Calvinist," and understood his Calvinism as a motivation to witness to his people group. He states, "Regeneration is the sole work of the Holy Spirit in the human heart and soul, and is in every case one and the same. Conversion, on the other hand, bringing into play the action also of the human will, is never absolutely the same perhaps in even two souls."[20]

Samuel Zwemer (1867-1952), an American Presbyterian missionary, called the "Apostle to Islam,"[21] was a Calvinist. A prolific writer, he penned "Calvinism and the Missionary Enterprise," an article that traces Calvinist missions and encourages Calvinists to go to the ends of the earth. In this article, he states that Calvin in the very beginning of his *magnum opus* provides a "great missionary principle" for those desiring to share the gospel. He also states that by that time Presbyterian churches had done more than one-quarter of the missions work in Islamic countries.[22]

Church's presence in Nigeria. See: John Piper, *You Will Be Eaten by Cannibals! Courage in the Cause of World Missions. Lessons in the Life of John G. Paton.* Audio cd. Minneapolis: Desiring God Ministries, 2000; and Johannes Verkuyl, "My Pilgrimage in Mission," *International Bulletin of Missionary Research* 10 no. 4 (October 1, 1986), 150.

19 John Piper, *You Will Be Eaten by Cannibals! Courage in the Cause of World Missions. Lessons in the Life of John G. Paton.* Audio cd. Minneapolis: Desiring God Ministries, 2000.

20 John G. Paton, *John G. Paton, D.D. Missionary to the New Hebrides: An Autobiography* (London: Hodder & Stoughton, 1891; reprint Adamant Media Corporation, 2005), 195, 372; in Google Books, <http://books.google.com/ books?id=Z6Vy7bH28R8C&pg=PA495&dq=John+G.+Paton:+Missionary+to+the+New+Hebredes,+An+Autobiography+Edited+by+His+Brother&ei=pA1fS6KgEaDiyQSyvLCYBA&cd=2#v=onepage&q=&f=false>, site editor, Google Books, accessed on 26 January 2010.

21 Christy J. Wilson, *Apostle to Islam: A Biography of Samuel M Zwemer* (New York: Friendship Press, 1970)

22 Samuel M. Zwemer, "Calvinism and the Missionary Enterprise," *Theology Today* 7, no. 2 (July 1950), 209, 215.

Era 3

In this period. if anything, there seems to be an increasing interest in Calvinism among some in the evangelical community.[23] Because Era 3 is relatively new, and many Calvinist missionaries from this era are still alive and serving on the field – some in dangerous places – little has been written from them or can be attributed to them. With that stated, there are many pastors, like Piper, who are Calvinists and promote missions, and many in their congregations are serving on the field. Two pastors and one denomination will be mentioned: Ascol, the late Tim Keller, and Sovereign Grace Ministries. Ascol, pastor of Grace Baptist Church, has been writing about Calvinism and missions for some time. More than one of the Founder's journals, which he created, has been dedicated to missions or has articles related to missions.[24] The church's focus in missions has been Central Asia, though Grace has sent people to Paraguay, Mexico, Greece, Romania, Brazil, China, Portugal, Guyana, Antigua, Zambia and South Africa.[25]

Keller, formerly the pastor of Redeemer Presbyterian Church in New York City, one of the most unreached places in the US, also was involved heavily in missions. In several messages, he addressed missions strategy and theology. In dealing with "Post-Christian"[26]

23   Jeff Robinson, "Study: Recent Grads 3 Times More Likely to be Calvinist," *Baptist Press* (November 27, 2007), <http://www.bpnews.net/bpnews.asp?id=26914>, site editor, Baptist Press, accessed on 29 January 2010, reports that a recent study of the largest Protestant denomination in the United States (the Southern Baptist Convention), shows a three-fold increase in Southern Baptist pastors who identify themselves as "5 Point Calvinists."

24   Founders Ministries, "Index," <http://www.founders.org/journal/index.html>, site editor, Founders Ministries, accessed on 29 January 2010.

25   Grace Baptist Church, "International," <http://www.truegraceofgod.org/missions/ international>, site editor, Grace Baptist Church, accessed on 29 January 2010.

26   This is my term. Tim Keller, "The Missional Church," <http://www.redeemer2.com/resources/papers/missional.pdf>, site editor, Redeemer Presbyterian Church, June 2001, accessed on 3 February 2010, defines this type of society as when "public institutions and popular culture [is]

societies, Keller provided a blueprint on how to reach them.[27] In discussing contextualization, he explained the importance of not losing the "offensive essentials" of the gospel while at the same time abandoning "any non-essential language or practice" that will offend the target group.[28] In speaking about people groups, Keller stated that Christians must "go to every ethnic group and bring them to be my [Christ's] followers."[29]

Sovereign Grace Ministries promotes Reformed (Calvinist) theology. Their stated goal is "planting and supporting local churches."[30] Concerning missions, Sovereign Grace's desire is to develop a team of workers that will advance their objectives cross-culturally: "[we desire to] export a biblical community that provides a compelling representation of the truth we proclaim.... In practical terms, our approach to missions often begins with posturing ourselves to serve and learn from Indigenous leaders who have expressed interest in Sovereign Grace.[31] There are Sovereign

---

no longer [a] 'Christianized' people, [but] the church still [runs] its ministries assuming that a stream of 'Christianized', traditional/moral people would simply show up in services."

27 Ibid. Keller states that Christians need to: talk in everyday language, understand the culture and use its elements to share the gospel; train people theologically to stay in public life; create a Christian community that is "counter-cultural and counter-intuitive;" and live out Christian unity at a locally as much as possible.

28 Tim Keller, "Advancing the Gospel into the 21st Century. Part III: Context Sensitive," <http://www.redeemer2.com/themovement/issues/2004/feb/advancingthegospel_3.html>, site editor, Redeemer Presbyterian Church, December 2003, accessed on 3 February 2010.

29 Tim Keller, "Advancing the Gospel into the 21st Century. Part II: Gospel-Centered," <http://www.redeemer2.com/themovement/issues/2003/dec/advancingthe gospel_2.html>, site editor, Redeemer Presbyterian Church, December 2003, accessed on 3 February 2010.

30 Sovereign Grace Ministries, "Who We Are," <http://www.sovgracemin.org/About/ AboutUs.aspx>, site editor, Sovereign Grace Ministries, accessed on 3 February 2010.

31 Sovereign Grace Ministries, " Church Planting Frequently Asked Questions," <http://www.SovereignGraceMinistries.org/ChurchPlanting/ChurchPlantingFAQ.aspx#08>, site editor, Sovereign Grace Ministries,

Grace workers in twenty-one countries including: Bolivia, Brazil, the UK, Germany, Ethiopia, India, Sri Lanka, Burma, Zambia, and South Korea.[32]

CONCLUSION

Calvinists are from varied groups with some being more theologically conservative and some having a higher quality of missiology than others. Most are missionaries, but some are (also) pastors and/or academics. The one common theme is that they stem from a Calvinist tradition that desires to see the gospel spread cross-culturally.

---

accessed on 3 February 2010.

32 Sovereign Grace Ministries, "We Plant & Build Local Churches with the Gospel: 2009-2010 Mission Update," <http://www.sovgracemin.org/Reference/Ministry Brochure%20web.pdf>, site editor, Sovereign Grace Ministries, accessed on 3 February 2010.

5

PIPER'S UNDERSTANDING OF THE MOTIVE AND NEED FOR MISSIONS

PIPER'S MOTIVATION FOR MISSIONS: WORSHIP OF GOD

Piper believes that God is the most important being in the universe.[1] God's passion for God's glory makes God the center of his own affections.[2] However, often God's importance is diminished and forgotten by those whose job dictates they exalt the glory of God.[3] Piper quotes scientist Charles Misner who comments how this failure affected Albert Einstein's understanding of Christianity:

> [Einstein] *must have looked at what the preachers said about God and felt that they were blaspheming. He had seen much more majesty than they had ever imagined, and they were just not talking about the real thing.* My guess is that

---

1   John Piper, "God is a Very Important Person," <http://www.desiringgod. org/library/topics/gods_passion/god_very_important.html>, site editor, Desiring God Ministries, October 31, 1984, accessed on 8 March 2004.

2   John Piper, "A Pastor's Role in World Missions," <http://www.desiring-god.org/ library/topics/pastors_role.html>, site editor, Desiring God Ministries, October 31, 1984, accessed on 3 March 2004. See also chapter 2.

3   John Piper, "Training the Next Generation of Evangelical Pastors and Missionaries," <http://www.desiringgod.org/library/topics/leadership/ train_next.html>, site editor, Desiring God Ministries, November 20, 1998, accessed on 5 March 2004.

he simply felt that religions he'd run across did not have the proper respect . . . for the author of the universe.[4]

Piper's understanding of God's importance in relation to missions is based on four factors: 1) God is committed to his fame and desires worship from all nations; 2) God's desire for worship is loving; 3) points one and two are the same; and 4) God's purposes cannot fail.[5]

Piper grounds his first conviction on his belief that the gospel must be preached to all nations before the end of history (Matt 24:14). Preaching the gospel to all peoples advances God's reputation and glory (Rom 9:17).[6] Piper questions Calvinists who maintain they cherish God's glory but fail to be missions minded. He states that the test of one's love for the glory of God rests in spreading God's glory by the proclamation of the gospel to all the nations.[7] One cannot be a "true Calvinist" unless he is missions minded.[8]

Piper's second conviction, God's desire to be worshiped is loving, is based on his belief that at the height of God's glory rests his mercy. God is merciful because he is the only one who can satisfy the human heart. When God glorifies himself, he magnifies his name and provides true joy for those who follow him. One aspect of God worshiping himself is God's love for himself. God loves himself more than any other being. If God failed to worship himself and love himself in this manner, joy would not be found in

---

4   Piper, "God is a Very Important Person," italics his.
5   John Piper and Tom Steller, "Driving Convictions Behind World Missions at Bethlehem," <http://bbcmpls.org>, site editor, Bethlehem Baptist Church, 1996, accessed on 1 March 2004. See also Piper, "Missions and the End of History."
6   Piper, "Missions and the End of History."
7   John Piper, "Driving Commands Behind World Missions at Bethlehem," <http://www.desiringgod.org/library/sermons/99/110296.html>, site editor, Desiring God Ministries, November 2, 1996, accessed on 4 March 2004.
8   Piper, *You Will Be Eaten by Cannibals!*

him, and God would be unloving to require worship. God's love is seen especially in Christ who came to earth to magnify the glory of God. Christ's mission shows God's promises are true, and provides a way for the nations to glorify God. Piper considers Christ the first missionary to an "unreached people group."[9]

Piper's third conviction, points one and two are the same, is based on Rom 15:9. When God becomes a person's true joy, God receives the glory, and the person gains the mercy of salvation. The glory of God and the salvation of man occur simultaneously. Isaiah 12:4, the "central command for world missions," states God's name needs to be proclaimed to all peoples in order that his name is praised among all nations.[10]

Piper's fourth conviction, God's purposes cannot fail, is based on God's will.[11] God's authority and sovereignty make Christ's word definite (Matt 24:35). Since Christ has been given power in heaven and earth (Matt 28:18), he promises to build his church (Matt 16:18) through believers and commands them to make disciples of all nations (Matt 28:19–20).[12] Christ paid the penalty for all his children and they are eternally secure. He predestined his children before the foundation of the earth (Eph 1:4) and they will be from every tribe, tongue, language, and people (Rev 5:9).[13] The end of time will come only after people from all people groups have received the gospel (Matt 24:14).[14]

Piper believes worship—honoring the glory of God by treasuring him above all things—should be everyone's motive for missions. He stresses this in a sermon about missions: "Unless we take our starting point from the sovereign majesty of God and his ultimate allegiance to his own glory above all else, our missionary theology and strategy and motivation will become human-centered

---

9   Piper, *Let the Nations Be Glad!*, 33.
10   Piper, "Driving Commands Behind World Missions at Bethlehem."
11   Ibid.
12   Piper, "Missions and the End of History."
13   Piper, "Driving Commands Behind World Missions at Bethlehem."
14   Piper, "Missions and the End of History."

and will in the end degenerate into a powerless sentimentality."[15] Only those who worship God will be properly inspired for missions because missions is the "overflow" of happiness in God.[16] In *Let the Nations Be Glad!,* Piper's most detailed work on missions, he further explains his belief that worship should be the church's goal and its motivation for missions:

> Missions is not the ultimate goal of the church. Worship is. Missions exists because worship doesn't. Worship is ultimate, not missions, because God is ultimate, not man. When this age is over, and countless millions of the redeemed fall on their faces before the throne of God, missions will be no more. It is a temporary necessity. But worship abides forever. . . . Missions is demanded not by God's failure to show glory but by man's failure to savor the glory. Creation is telling the glory of God, but the peoples are not treasuring it.[17]

Missions fills the world with "white-hot worshipers" of God from all people groups.[18] The only question regarding the motivation for missions is human participation. God's revealed will is not accomplished unless Christians proclaim the gospel to every

---

15   John Piper, "A Pastor's Role in World Missions."

16   Piper, *Let the Nations Be Glad!,* 21.

17   Ibid., 17, 205. This is also stated in John Piper, "Affirmation of Faith," <http://www.desiringgod.org/library/what_we_believe/tbi_affirmation. html>, site editor, Desiring God Ministries, August 28, 2000, accessed on 6 June 2003. This is Bethlehem Baptist Church's Affirmation of Faith. Piper, *Let the Nations Be Glad!,* 215–38, goes to great lengths to explain his desire is not for people to be won to Christ in order that they attend corporate worship. While this is important, it is too provincial and limited. Piper desires Christian worship to be "radical and soul-gripping and life-encompassing," much broader than worship on Sunday and Wednesday nights. See Piper, *Desiring God,* 77–111.

18   John Piper, "Prayer: The Work of Missions," <http://desiringgod.org/ library/topics/ prayer/prayer_missions.html>, site editor, Desiring God Ministries, October 30, 1983, accessed on 16 January 2004.

people. If one fails to proclaim the message of salvation, God will "pass [him] over" and do his work through another.[19]

THE NEED FOR MISSIONS: SALVATION THROUGH CHRIST ALONE

While Piper's motive for missions is worship, missions is needed because salvation is through Christ alone. He affirms the reality and eternity of hell, the necessity of Christ's atonement, and the necessity for people to have conscious faith in Christ for salvation.

The Reality and Eternity of Hell

Piper maintains the doctrine of eternal hell is essential to Christianity. He cites writer Dorothy Sayers who states that one cannot deny this reality without "tearing the New Testament to tatters [and] altogether repudiating Christ."[20] Piper himself states, "Until we feel some measure of dread about God's future [eternal] wrath, we will probably never grasp the sweetness with which the early church savored the saving work of Christ."[21] Piper cites annihilationist theologians Clark Pinnock and John Stott as representatives for those who disagree.[22] Pinnock[23] and Stott[24] use similar arguments in their defense of annihilationism. They are not dogmatic about their position though they desire it to become

---

19   Piper, "Missions and the End of History."

20   Dorothy Sayers, *A Matter of Eternity*, ed. Rosamond Kent Sprague (Grand Rapids: Eerdmans, 1973), 86; quoted in John Piper, *Pierced by the Word* (Sisters, OR: Multnomah, 2003), 49.

21   John Piper, *The Passion of Jesus Christ* (Wheaton: Crossway, 2004), 113.

22   Piper, *Let the Nations Be Glad!*, 112 n 3, 120 n 15.

23   Clark Pinnock, "The Destruction of the Finally Impenitent," *Criswell Theological Review* 4, no. 2 (Spring 1990): 243–59; and Clark Pinnock, "The Conditional View," in *Four Views of Hell*, ed. William Crockett (Grand Rapids: Zondervan, 1992), 135–66.

24   David L. Edwards and John Stott, *Evangelical Essentials: A Liberal - Evangelical Dialogue* (Downers Grove, IL: InterVarsity, 1988), 306–29.

another recognized option in evangelical circles.[25] Their main argument from Scripture rests on the understanding of the term "destruction," which they maintain means annihilation.[26]

Pinnock argues that the Old Testament provides the metaphors the New Testament uses for hell. He cites Ps 37 that asserts the wicked will disappear as the grass and be annihilated. He also cites Mal 4:1–2 that maintains there will be nothing left to the evil person.[27] In the New Testament, Pinnock explains that Matt 10:28 states that Christ will destroy the wicked one's soul in hell. Pinnock believes "destroy" means annihilation because John the Baptist uses the term to mean annihilate when he parallels the wicked as dry wood thrown into an "unquenchable fire." Further, Pinnock explains that Christ states that sinners will be cast into Gehenna (Matt 5:30), a place where garbage may have burned during Christ's day. The idea is that the unregenerate, like the garbage, will be annihilated. Pinnock believes that Paul alludes to annihilation when Paul states that God will destroy the wicked in 1 Cor 3:17 and Phil 1:28. Pinnock believes this idea is true in every other New Testament book.[28] Pinnock provides several other reasons why he disagrees with the traditional understanding of hell. He states that God sending people to everlasting torment makes God's justice vengeance, instead of punishment. He quotes Hans Küng:

> Even apart from the image of a truly merciless God that contradicts everything we can assume from what Jesus says of the Father of the lost, can we be surprised at a

---

25   Ibid., 320; Pinnock, The Destruction of the Finally Impenitent," 259; and Pinnock, "The Conditional View," 162.

26   Pinnock and Stott also believe the idea of an eternal soul for everyone is a Greek concept rather than biblical one. See Edwards and Stott, *Evangelical Essentials*, 316; Pinnock, "The Destruction of the Finally Impenitent," 252; and Pinnock, "The Conditional View," 148.

27   Pinnock, "The Destruction of the Finally Impenitent," 251; and Pinnock, "The Conditional View," 145.

28   Ibid., 251; and Ibid., 146. Pinnock cites other verses like the ones mentioned: 2 Thes 1:9, Gal 6:8, Rom 1:32, 6:23, and Phil 3:19.

time when retributive punishments without an opportunity of probation are being increasingly abandoned in
education and penal justice that the idea not only of a
lifelong, but even eternal punishment of the body and
soul, seem to many people absolutely monstrous.[29]

The idea of eternal torment creates dualism and disagrees
with passages that state God is the "all in all" (1 Cor 15:28, Rev
21:5).[30] Pinnock also examines proof texts of the traditional understanding. The only passage that he credits with having merit
to the traditional argument is Matt 25:46. He believes this text
allows for either interpretation.[31]

Stott gives four reasons for his belief that destruction means
annihilation: language, imagery, justice, and universalism. He believes language in Scripture indicates that to destroy is to kill or
perish, not eternally to torment. He states, "If to kill is to deprive
the body of life, hell would seem to be the depravation of both
physical and spiritual life, that is the extinction of being. . . . It
would seem strange, therefore, if people who are said to suffer
destruction are in fact not destroyed."[32] His understanding of
imagery focuses on the idea of eternal fire. The purpose of fire is
not to bring pain, but to destroy. The idea of "consuming fire" or
"unquenchable fire" (Matt 3:12, Luke 3:17) indicates that what is
placed in the fire is "consumed for ever [sic], not tormented for
ever [sic]."[33] His idea of God's justice concentrates on the belief
that God will punish sin appropriately and proportionately (Rev
20:12). Condemning humans to eternal hell for finite sin is un-
balanced punishment. His idea involves passages in Scripture that

29 Hans Küng, *Eternal Life, Life After Death as a Medical, Philosophical, and
    Theological Problem* (New York: Doubleday, 1984), 136–37; quoted in
    Pinnock, The Destruction of the Finally Impenitent," 255; and Pinnock,
    "The Conditional View," 153.

30 Pinnock, "The Destruction of the Finally Impenitent," 255; and Pin-
    nock, "The Conditional View," 154.

31 Ibid., 256; and Ibid., 155–58.

32 Edwards and Stott, *Evangelical Essentials*, 315–16.

33 Ibid., 316.

state God will be "everything to everybody" (1 Cor 15:28). He maintains God will be victorious over evil and will draw all men to himself (John 12:32) by annihilating unbelievers. He thinks this understanding of hell is more compatible with the universal reign of God.[34]

Piper maintains these defenses of annihilationism are incorrect and unproven in Scripture. He believes the Old and New Testaments depict hell as eternal. Daniel 12:2 states that some after death will be sent to "everlasting life" and some to "everlasting contempt." The Hebrew word for everlasting, *'olam*, in the context of the verse, means "forever" because there is a separation between joy and pain after death. Piper concludes: "As the *life* is everlasting, so the shame and *contempt are everlasting*."[35]

As Christ, who uses the term more than anyone,[36] describes hell as an "unquenchable fire" (Mark 9:43–48), Piper asks, if annihilation is the idea in Mark 9:48, why is stress placed on the idea of "fire never being quenched and the worm never dying?"[37] Further, Matt 18:8 states that the fire is "eternal" and Matt 25:41, 46 demonstrates the eternal fire of hell is the eternal punishment for the unbeliever, as heaven is eternal life for the Christian. He connects Matt 25:41, 46, to Rev 20:10 where the beast and false prophet are sent to eternal destruction. He responds to claims that Rev 20:10 does not discuss ordinary humans by citing Rev 20:15, 21:8, and 14:10. All these texts state that individuals will be sent to hell forever to experience "eternal conscious torment." The strongest Greek term for eternity, eis *aióonas aiónón*, "unto ages of ages," is used to describe hell in Rev 19:3, 20:10,[38] and Rev 20:15 and 21:8 state that hell is meant for the lost.[39]

---

34   Ibid., 318–19.

35   Piper, *Let the Nations Be Glad!*, 116, italics his.

36   John Piper, *Seeing and Savoring Jesus Christ* (Wheaton, IL: Crossway, 2001), 102, 125.

37   Piper, *Let the Nations Be Glad!*, 116–17.

38   In Rev 20:20, the term is *eis tous aiónas tón aiónón*, "unto the ages of the ages."

39   Piper, *Let the Nations Be Glad!*, 116–20.

Piper agrees that the term "destruction" in Matt 10:28 means "final;" however, he believes destruction means final "eternal ruin," not annihilation.[40] He questions the purpose of Matt 26:24 that Judas would be better off not even being born, if he is only annihilated. If the annihilationist claim is true, then annihilationism is an act of God's grace instead of punishment.[41] He quotes Edwards' response to the argument that eternity in hell is not appropriate for finite sin. Edwards explains humans are under command to love an infinite God; failing this task makes humans "infinitely faulty." Therefore, sin against God is "a violation of infinite obligations, [it] must be a crime infinitely heinous, and so deserving infinite punishment."[42]

God demands humans thank him and manifest his glory.[43] A person's failure to follow these commands leads to punishment in hell forever;[44] a place where God "vindicates the wrath of his glory in holy wrath on those who would not delight in what is infinitely glorious."[45] Unless a person knows his true destination apart from Christ, he may be lured to a false gospel.[46] Belief in an eternal hell over the annihilationist position makes a "tremendous difference" in missions because, "The difference between not

---

40   Ibid., 117.

41   John Piper, "God Did Not Spare His Own Son," <http://www.desiring-god.org/library/ sermons/02/081802.html>, site editor, Desiring God Ministries, August 18, 2002, accessed on 29 March 2004.

42   Jonathan Edwards, "The Justice of God in the Damnation of Sinners," in *The Works of Jonathan Edwards*, vol. 1 (Edinburgh: Banner of Truth, 1974), 669; quoted in Piper, "Conversion: The Creation of a Christian Hedonist," <http://www.desiringgod.org/ dg/id36_m.htm>, site editor, Desiring God Ministries, accessed on 31 March 2004.

43   John Piper, "The Wrath of God Against Ungodliness and Unrighteousness [Part 2]," <http://www.desiringgod.org/library/sermons/98/091398.html>, site editor, Desiring God Ministries, September 13, 1998, accessed on 25 March 2004.

44   John Piper, "God Credits Faith as Righteousness," <http://www.desiring-god.org/ library/sermons/99/080199.html>, site editor, Desiring God Ministries, August 1, 1999, accessed on 29 March 2004.

45   Piper, *God's Passion for His Glory*, 38.

46   Piper, "God Credits Faith as Righteousness."

existing and existing in torment for ever [sic] is an infinite differ-ence."[47]

The Necessity of Christ's Atonement

Piper believes Christ's atonement is foundational to missions. Salvation is a result of Christ substituting himself for humankind's sin.[48] Piper cites pluralist John Hick and universalist George MacDonald as representatives who disagree.[49] Hick does not believe in the atonement because he does not believe Christ is God or claimed to be God. Hick thinks belief in the incarnation is a "mythical idea,"[50] calls it a tautology,[51] and an "arbitrary superiority-by-definition" explanation that provides unwarranted exclusiveness to Christianity.[52] He redefines and renames salvation to "salvation/liberation," a "change in men and women from natural self-centeredness . . . to a new orientation in the Ultimate, the Real, as conceived within one's own tradition."[53] Salvation/liberation includes all faiths, even those that promote impersonal deities.[54]

---

47   John Piper, "Behold the Kindness and the Severity of God: The Echo and Insufficiency of Hell Part One," <http://www.desiringgod.org/library/sermons/92/ 061492.html>, site editor, Desiring God Ministries, June 21, 1992, accessed on 1 April 2004.

48   Piper, *Let the Nations Be Glad!*, 125.

49   Ibid., 113; and Piper, *The Pleasures of God*, 172–74, respectively.

50   John Hick, "Whatever Path Men Choose is Mine," in *Christianity and Other Religions: Selected Readings*, eds. John Hick and Brian Hebblewaite (Philadelphia: Fortress, 1980), 186.

51   John Hick, "A Pluralist View," in *More than One Way: Four Views of Salvation in a Pluralistic World*, eds. Dennis Okholm and Timothy R. Phillips (Grand Rapids: Zondervan, 1995), 43.

52   John Hick, "The Non-Absoluteness of Christianity," in *The Myth of Christian Uniqueness: Towards a Pluralistic Theology of Religions*, eds. John Hick and Paul F. Knitter (Maryknoll: Orbis, 1987), 23.

53   John Hick, "The Theological Challenge of Religious Pluralism," in *Christianity and Other Religions: Selected Readings*, rev. and ed. John Hick and Brian Hebblewaite (Oxford: Oneworld, 2001), 164.

54   Hick, "A Pluralist View," 43–44.

MacDonald argues that the New Testament does not discuss the traditional, evangelical understanding of the atonement. He states there is no "word in the New Testament about reconciling God to us; it is we that have to be reconciled to God."[55] The death of Christ serves as an encouragement to acknowledge sin and repent; the atonement is a person's payment to God for his evil actions. This idea leads MacDonald to believe that everyone will eventually receive Christ and go to heaven, even those in hell. He does not believe that a person can sin to the point of God sending him to hell for eternity. He states that if that were correct, then "God remains defeated, for he has created that which sinned, and which would not repent and make up for its sin."[56]

Piper does not believe Scripture supports either argument. He does not debate Hick directly; however, he refers to some works that address Hick's position[57] and presents a biblical defense of the deity of Christ.[58] Piper focuses on Scriptures that relate to the atonement. Romans 5:17–19 and 1 Cor 15:21–23 characterize Christ's death and resurrection in relation to Adam. Adam represents the federal head for humankind, and Christ rep-

---

55 George MacDonald, "Justice," in *George MacDonald: Creation in Christ*, ed. Rolland Hein (Wheaton: Harold Shaw, 1976), 78.

56 Ibid., 74.

57 Piper, *Let the Nations Be Glad!*, 113 n 4. Piper cites the following work by Hick: John Hick, "Whatever Path Men Choose is Mine," in *Christianity and Other Religions*, ed. John Hick and Brian Hebblethwaite (Philadelphia: Fortress, 1980). Piper also provides two other works that give an overview of Hick's thought: Harold Netland, *Dissonant Voices: Religious Pluralism and the Question of Truth* (1991; reprint, Vancouver: Regent Publishers, 1998) and Harold Netland, *Encountering Religious Pluralism: The Challenge to Christian Faith and Mission* (Downers Grove, IL: InterVarsity, 2001).

58 For example: John Piper, "Jesus is the Christ the Son of God," <http://www.desiringgod.org/library/sermons/91/100691.html>, site editor, Desiring God Ministries, October 6, 1991, accessed on 22 April 2004; John Piper, "Jesus is the Christ the Son of God," <http://www.desiringgod.org/library/topics/christ/the_ unparalleled_passion_of_jesus_ christ. html>, site editor, Desiring God Ministries, accessed on 22 April 2004; Piper, *Desiring God*, 236–31; and Piper, *The Pleasures of God*, 34–42.

resents the federal head for believers. As Adam's sin is imputed on his posterity (humankind), Christ's act of grace is imputed on his posterity (believers); Christ has become sin for believers and taken their judgment upon himself (2 Cor 5:21).[59] The book of Revelation as a whole distinguishes Christ as "King of kings and Lord of lords."[60] Revelation 5:9, for instance, explains that by Christ's blood he bought people from every tribe, language, people, and nation.[61]

In response to MacDonald, Piper states MacDonald's position is a "massive reinterpretation of biblical teaching concerning the cross."[62] Piper does not believe the death of Christ serves just as an example or an encouragement to repent of sin. The death of Christ serves as the manner that God forgives man. Romans 3:25–26 states that God reconciles humans to himself to display his glory.[63] God redirects his furor toward Christ at the cross. Christ has become the propitiation for the Christian's sin and enables him to stand righteously before God.[64] Piper quotes theo-

---

59   John Piper, "Adam, Christ, and Justification: Part Two," <http://www.desiringgod.org/ library/sermons/00/062500.html>, site editor, Desiring God Ministries, June 25, 2000, accessed on 22 April 2004; and Piper, *Let the Nations Be Glad!*, 123.

60   Piper, *Let the Nations Be Glad!*, 124.

61   John Piper, "Every Race to Reign and Worship," <http://www.desiringgod.org/library/ sermons/98/011898.html>, site editor, Desiring God Ministries, January 18, 1998, accessed on 23 April 2004. See also John Piper, "God's Pursuit of Racial Diversity At Infinite Cost," <http://www.desiringgod.org/library/sermons/01/ 011401.html>, site editor, Desiring God Ministries, January 14, 2001, accessed on 23 April 2004; and Piper, *Let the Nations Be Glad!*, 124. While not in Revelation, Luke 24:46–47 maintains that because of Christ's death and resurrection, the gospel should be proclaimed to all peoples. See: Piper, *Let the Nations Be Glad!*, 125. In 125 n 22, Piper provides many other Scripture references that state Christ's atonement is necessary for salvation.

62   Piper, *The Pleasures of God*, 173.

63   Piper, *The Justification of God*, 150. See also John Piper, "The Demonstration of the Righteousness of God," *Journal for the Study of the New Testament* 7 (April 1980): 2–32.

64   John Piper, "Jesus is Precious Because He Removes Our Guilt," <http://

logian William Childs Robinson to show the biblical necessity of reconciliation by the cross:

> Man's rebellious enmity against God (Colossians 1:12; Romans 8:7f) has called forth his holy enmity against evil (1 Corinthians 15:25ff; Romans 11:28; James 4:4); his wrath (Romans 1:18; 2:5, 8–9; Ephesians 2:3, 5; Colossians 3:6); his judgments (Romans 1:24–32; 2:3, 16; 3:6, 19; 2 Corinthians 5:10); his vengeance (Romans 12:19; 2 Thessalonians 2:8); and the curse of the broken law (Galatians 3:10). The wrath of God in the final judgment stands in immediate connection with the enmity which is removed by the reconciliation (Romans 5:9–10). This God so acted in giving his Son to be made sin and a curse for us that his wrath was averted and his righteousness made manifest even in forgiving believers (Romans 3:25–26). The grace of the Lord Jesus Christ assures them that the sentence of condemnation is no longer against them.[65]

The Need for Conscious Faith in Christ for Salvation

Piper believes salvation only occurs when a person places his faith in Christ. Those who never hear the gospel spend eternity in hell.[66] He explains there are various positions on the fate of the

---

www.desiringgod.org/library/sermons/82/022182.html>, site editor, Desiring God Ministries, February 21, 1982, accessed on 22 April 2004; and Piper, *The Pleasures of God*, 163–65.

65 William Childs Robinson, "Reconciliation," quoted in *Baker's Dictionary of Theology*, ed. Everett F. Harrison (Grand Rapids: Baker, 1960), 437–38; in Piper, *The Pleasures of God*, 173–74.

66 Piper, *Let the Nations Be Glad!*, 133 n 27, believes there is an exception made for the salvation of babies and the mentally disabled who cannot comprehend any type of revelation, general or specific. He cites Rom 1:20 and states, "The Bible does not deal with this special case in any detail, and we are left to speculate that the fitness of the connection between faith in Christ and salvation will be preserved through the coming to faith of children whenever God brings them to maturity in heaven or

unevangelized. Some, like Stott, remain agnostic.[67] Others such as Pinnock,[68] state that unevangelized, pietistic individuals from other religions can be saved like the Old Testament believers. Still others like evangelical theologians Millard Erickson[69] and A. H. Strong[70] modify the position Pinnock holds and state that there may be a possibility for salvation for those who never hear the gospel like believers in the Old Testament. Erickson and Pinnock will be used to represent this position.[71]

Erickson believes some who never hear the gospel may be saved in the same way people in the Old Testament received salvation, through general revelation without knowing the name of Jesus. He reasons that if salvation could happen for those who never heard about Christ in the Old Testament era, could it be true for those who never heard about Christ in the New Testament? He answers, "The basis of acceptance would be the work of Jesus Christ, even though the person involved is not conscious that this is how provision has been made for his or her salvation."[72] He disagrees with the explanation that in the Old Testament, Christ

---

in the age to come." In this note, he provides many works that defend this position.

67   Edwards and Stott, *Evangelical Essentials*, 327; quoted in Piper, *Let the Nations Be Glad!*, 113 n 5.

68   Clark Pinnock, "Acts 4:12—No Other Name Under Heaven," in *Through No Fault of Their Own*, eds. William Crockett and James G. Sigountos (Grand Rapids: Baker, 1991), 113; quoted in Piper, *Let the Nations Be Glad!*, 125 n 23.

69   Millard Erickson, "Hope for Those Who Haven't Heard? Yes, But . . . ," *Evangelical Missions Quarterly* 11, no. 2 (April 1975): 124–25; quoted in Piper, *Let the Nations Be Glad!*, 114 n 7.

70   A. H. Strong, *Systematic Theology* (Westwood, NJ: Revell, 1907), 842; quoted in Piper, *Let the Nations Be Glad!*, 114 n 7.

71   There are crucial differences between Pinnock and Erickson, and they different markedly on just how far they are willing to go. However, since Piper, *Let the Nations Be Glad!*, 112–14, cites both of them as antagonists toward his position, both will be used.

72   Millard Erickson, *Christian Theology*, 2d ed. (Grand Rapids: Baker, 1998), 197. See also Millard Erickson, *How Shall They Be Saved? The Destiny of Those Who Do Not Hear of Jesus* (Grand Rapids: Baker, 1996).

had yet to come and in the New Testament, he has already come. Erickson believes that since God is not bound by time, events do not have to be viewed in succession. He questions the need for the unevangelized to hear the gospel:

> If Jews possessed salvation in the Old Testament era simply by virtue of having the form of the Christian gospel without its content, can this principle be extended? Could it be that those who ever since the time of Christ have had no opportunity to hear the gospel, as it has come through the special revelation, participate in this salvation on the same basis?[73]

Erickson quotes Strong to strengthen his argument:

> The patriarchs, though they had not knowledge of a personal Christ, were saved by believing in God so far as God had revealed himself to them; and whoever among the heathen are saved, must in like manner be saved by casting themselves as helpless sinners upon God's plan of mercy, dimly shadowed forth in nature and providence.[74]

Erickson states that hearing about Christ is not necessary for salvation, although salvation is found in the death and resurrection of Christ. According to Rom 10:18 (a quotation from Ps 19:4), a person can hear the gospel through general revelation. Romans 1–3 demonstrates that God reveals attributes about himself to every person in nature. Through general revelation a person can know God exists, that God is "powerful," "creative," "holy," and "moral;" and that he expects humans to act in a particular manner. A person is "without excuse" because these characteristics are "written on [his] heart." To receive the gospel, Erickson believes a person must know that God is good and powerful, and that God's law requires obedience. A person must also realize that he is guilty and that he does not meet God's standards; he can do

---

73 Erickson, "Hope for Those Who Haven't Heard?," 125.

74 Strong, *Systematic Theology*, 842; quoted in Erickson, "Hope for Those Who Haven't Heard?," 123

nothing to atone for his sin; and God will forgive those who beg for his mercy. [75]

Pinnock, more strongly than Erickson, believes the unevangelized can be saved. He thinks the notion that God would send the unevangelized to hell is "cruel and offensive." He questions the character of a God who sends people to hell "without the remotest chance of responding to his truth."[76] Since God loves the world and wants everyone to receive salvation, everyone has access to the gospel. A person is judged based on what he knows and can only respond to the revelation he has received.[77] All a person needs for salvation is faith (Heb 11:6).[78] Salvation occurs for the unevangelized in the same way it occurred for Old Testament people such as Abel, Noah, Enoch, and Job who were neither Christian nor Jew and did not know the name of Jesus. He quotes Rom 2:6 and states, "Obviously the unevangelized can be saved by faith just like anyone else."[79]

Pinnock explains that the story of Cornelius in Acts 10 is one of the most compelling examples of a lost person becoming saved before receiving Christ. Pinnock compares Cornelius with Job and calls him a "pagan saint" who had an "acceptable relationship with God" outside the Christian and Jewish community.[80] Pinnock explains that Acts 10:34–35 states that God accepts those who place their faith in him regardless of race and religion. He believes there are only three requirements for a pagan to be saved: 1) he must fear God; 2) he must seek righteousness in his behavior; and 3)

---

75 Erickson, "Hope for Those Who Haven't Heard?," 123–25.

76 Clark Pinnock, *A Wideness of God's Mercy: The Finality of Jesus Christ in a World of Religions* (Grand Rapids: Zondervan, 1992), 153–54.

77 Ibid., 159–62.

78 Ibid., 159, 161. See also Clark Pinnock, "An Inclusivist View," in *More Than One Way: Four Views of Salvation in a Pluralistic World*, eds. Dennis Okholm and Timothy R. Phillips (Grand Rapids: Zondervan, 1995), 117.

79 Pinnock, *A Wideness of God's Mercy*, 161.

80 Ibid., 92, 94.

he must have faith. These essentials are seen in Noah's, Abraham's, and Jesus' covenant. All three focus on faith.[81]

Pinnock argues with those who maintain that Acts 4:12 means that one needs to know the name of Jesus for salvation. He believes salvation occurs only through faith in Christ but understands that Acts 4:12 does not discuss the fate of the unevangelized or explain God's plan to use other religions in redemption. Faulty presuppositions bring those ideas into the text.[82]

Pinnock does not believe his position hinders missions. He explains that Abraham was justified by faith and did not hear the name of Jesus, but Paul witnessed to Abraham's descendants because they needed to know the "fullness of salvation." When possible, every unevangelized "Christian" should understand the origin of their salvation.[83] He believes his position should motivate missions to unreached people groups because God is already in these places. When missionaries arrive "we call them [the unevangelized persons who are saved] to come higher up and deeper in, to know God better and love God more."[84]

Piper maintains that Scripture demonstrates that God sends those who never hear the name of Jesus to hell. Before the incarnation, people were in times of ignorance because God did not reveal the mystery of Christ. The mystery of Christ is that Gentiles are heirs with Israel in Christ and that their inheritance comes only through the gospel.[85] God did not make salvation known clearly to the nations until the incarnation because God wanted Christ to be the focus of worship.[86] The times of ignorance were part of God's sovereign will to keep salvation from the nations and allow them to continue in their rebellion. Before the incarnation, people

---

81 Ibid., 105.
82 Pinnock, "Acts 4:12," 109, 113.
83 Ibid., 114.
84 Pinnock, "An Inclusivist View," 120.
85 John Piper, "The Cosmic Church," <http://www.desiringgod.org/library/sermons/81/032281.html>, site editor, Desiring God Ministries, March 22, 1981, accessed on 9 April 2004.
86 Piper, *Let the Nations Be Glad!*, 127–29.

were saved by placing faith in the mercy of God. They trusted his miraculous works in the exodus, the sacrificial system, and the promise of a savior. However, they did not know the name of Jesus, nor understand that people from all people groups would receive salvation, nor that all people groups would be equal heirs with the Jews in the kingdom of heaven.[87]

The times of ignorance ceased with the incarnation of Christ. Now God commands all people from all nations to place their faith in Christ (Acts 17:30–31).[88] God commands those who believe to share the gospel with all people groups. All people everywhere must confess with their mouth that Jesus is Lord and believe in their heart that God raised him from the dead (Rom 10:9).

Piper does not believe those who hold positions like Pinnock and Erickson see the coming of Christ as the decisive event in redemptive history. Cornelius was lost until Peter shared Christ with him. Acts 11:14 shows that the gospel is essential for salvation. In Acts 10:43, Peter states everyone who believes in Christ "receives forgiveness of sins from his name." Peter went to Cornelius in order that he could understand that forgiveness comes through Christ, not to tell him that God has forgiven his sins. When Peter tells the Jewish Christians the reason he went to a Gentile in Acts 11:18, their reservations about a Jew associating with a Gentile are calmed. Further, other places in Acts (Acts 2:5, 3:19, 13:38–39) call devout people to salvation.[89] Regarding Acts 10:35, Piper understands Cornelius as a representation of a person from an unreached people group who is searching for God in an

---

87   John Piper, "The Age of Ignorance Is Over," <http://www.desiringgod. org/library/ sermons/87/062187.html>, site editor, Desiring God Ministries, June 21, 1987, accessed on 9 April 2004.

88   Ibid.

89   John Piper, "What God Has Cleansed Do Not Call Common," <http:// www.desiringgod.org/library/sermons/91/102091.html>, site editor, Desiring God Ministries, October 20, 1991, accessed on 12 April 2004. See also Piper, *Let the Nations Be Glad!*, 135–36.

exceptional manner. God faithfully sends a missionary to him so he can receive the gospel.[90]

Piper also disagrees with Pinnock's interpretation of Acts 4:12. Piper explains that Pinnock fails to understand the importance of Peter's focus on the name of Jesus.[91] Commenting on Acts 1:8, Piper states, "There is no other source of saving power that you can be saved by under some OTHER name. . . . His name is our entrance into fellowship with God. The way of salvation by faith is a way that brings glory to the name of Jesus."[92] In his remarks on Acts 10:43, he states forgiveness is found only in believing in the name of Jesus.[93] Likewise, he emphasizes salvation in Christ alone in discussing Rom 10:11–15. Romans 10:11, a quotation from Isa 28:16, and Rom 10:13, a quotation from Joel 2:32, are references to Christ; no one will be ashamed if he calls on Christ, believes in him, and confesses that he is Lord.[94] Paul raises three important questions concerning the unevangelized in Rom 10:14–15:1: 1) how shall a person call on Christ whose name he does not believe?; 2) how shall a person believe in Christ whose name he does not know?; and 3) how shall a person know Christ without someone telling him? Question one assumes the one calling has faith in the one on whom he calls, which disagrees with those who state that a person can call on God without knowing the name of Jesus. Question two presumes the gospel must include hearing Christ, which denies the idea that God can save a person without knowing Christ. Question three supposes there must be a Christian to

90 Ibid.; and Ibid., 136–39, respectively.

91 Piper, *Let the Nations Be Glad!*, 141.

92 John Piper, "There is Salvation in No One Else," <http://www.desiring-god.org/ library/sermons/91/012091.html>, site editor, Desiring God Ministries, January 20, 1991, accessed on 12 April 2004.

93 Ibid.; and Piper, *Let the Nations Be Glad!*, 141.

94 John Piper, "The Word of Faith We Proclaim: Part Two," <http://www.desiringgod.org/library/sermons/03/052503.html>, site editor, Desiring God Ministries, March 25, 2003, accessed on 13 April 2004. See also John Piper, "The Word of Faith We Proclaim: Part One," <http://www.desiring god.org/library/sermons/03/ 051803.html>, site editor, Desiring God Ministries, March 18, 2003, accessed on 13 April 2004.

tell the unevangelized about Christ.[95] Piper believes that Erickson fails to understand correctly the order of the events when Erickson claims that Ps 19:4 (Rom 10:18) states that salvation can occur from general revelation alone. Piper explains that Erickson's position on Rom 10:18 makes Paul's questions in Rom 10:14 "misleading."[96] Piper argues that the gospel has been preached to Israel, she has refused it, and is responsible for her rejection. Whether this is in the context of Ps19:4 and whether it refers to general revelation or is just an example of the gospel being presented for Israel to make a response is not the main point.[97]

Further, Piper cites Paul and John's motivation to preach the gospel to unreached peoples as evidence that God requires the name of Jesus to be proclaimed for salvation to occur. Both John and Paul state people must believe in Christ (Rom 10:14; John 10:27). Both maintain that unbelievers hear Christ's voice when Christians proclaim the gospel to them (Rom 10:14; John 17:20–21). Both believe that God saves his elect from all over the world (Rom 15:15–18; Rev 5:9–10).[98]

Piper states that believing the unreached may enter heaven hinders missions. He compares the statistics of missions in mainline denominations that espouse this position with those of evangelical Protestants who maintain that conscious faith in Christ is needed for salvation. From 1953–1980, the number of missionaries in mainline denominations decreased from 9,044 to 2,813, while the number of evangelical Protestants missionaries increased by 200 percent. The Christian and Missionary Alliance, with a

---

95   Piper, *Let the Nations Be Glad!*, 145. See also John Piper, "How Shall People Be Saved [Part One]," <http://www.desiring god.org/library/ sermons/03/060103.html>, site editor, Desiring God Ministries, June 1, 2003, accessed on 13 April 2004. See also John Piper, "How Shall People Be Saved: Part Two," <http://www.desiringgod.org/library/ sermons/03/083103.html>, site editor, Desiring God Ministries, August 31, 2003, accessed on 13 April 2004.

96   Piper, *Let the Nations Be Glad!*, 146.

97   Piper, "How Shall People Be Saved: Part Two."

98   Piper, *Let the Nations Be Glad!*, 149–52.

membership of 220,000, supports forty percent more missionaries than the United Methodist Church with its 9.5 million members.[99]

---

99 Piper, *Desiring God*, 228.

6

PIPER'S UNDERSTANDING OF THE GOAL OF MISSIONS:

PEOPLE GROUPS, NOT INDIVIDUALS

Piper's understanding of the goal and need of missions flows from his belief that God's glory is manifested when people from all nations worship him. Salvation comes only through the atonement of Christ and can only be given to those who consciously place their faith in Christ. Those who reject Christ stay in their sin and upon death suffer in hell for eternity. The goal of missions is reaching all people groups for Christ rather than individuals. Pain and suffering in the missionary enterprise, while not part of the goal of missions, necessarily work alongside cross-cultural evangelism and complete what is "lacking" in Christ's own afflictions.

THE GREAT COMMISSION:
PEOPLE GROUPS, NOT INDIVIDUALS

Old Testament

Piper believes that Scripture pictures the Great Commission's task as reaching people groups rather than individuals for Christ. He notes that the Great Commission is found throughout the Old Testament. There is a confidence that all people groups will worship Christ, especially in Psalms and Isaiah. Piper divides the passages in Psalms and Isaiah into four groups.[1] In the first set of passages, God commands his glory be proclaimed to all people groups. Psalm 96:3–4 charges that God's glory must be spoken

---

1   Piper, *Desiring God*, 70–74.

to the nations to magnify his greatness.[2] Isaiah 12:4 states, "Make known [God's] deeds among the peoples, *proclaim that his name is exalted.*"[3] Psalm 117:1 (LXX) calls all the nations, *panta ta ethné* the same phrase used in Matt 28:18–20, to praise God.[4] The reason for the nations' praise is God's love toward Israel because through Israel, God will send the Savior, Jesus Christ.[5]

In the second set of passages, God promises that all people groups will worship him. Isaiah 52:15 maintains all peoples will hear the gospel, and kings will be in awe that the one who suffered on the cross is now exalted before God.[6] Psalm 86:9 guarantees that God will convert the nations to worship and glorify his name.[7] Isaiah 55:5 makes clear that God's call of salvation to the

---

2   John Piper, "That All the Nations Might Hear," <http://www.desiring-god. org/library/sermons/00/102900.html>, site editor, Desiring God Ministries, October 29, 2000, accessed on 18 May 2004; and John Piper, "Every Race to Reign and Worship," <http://www.desiringgod.org/ library/sermons/98/011898.html>, site editor, Desiring God Ministries, January 18, 1998, accessed on 18 May 2004.

3   Piper, "Driving Convictions Behind World Missions At Bethlehem." See also Piper, "Missions and the End of History," italics his.

4   John Piper, "Everlasting Truth for the Joy of All Peoples," <http://www. desiringgod.org/library/sermons/03/102603.html>, site editor, Desiring God Ministries, October 26, 2003, accessed on 14 May 2004. Piper states that the parallel between Gentiles, *goim*, and peoples, *ha'umin*, indicates that people groups are being discussed, not Gentile individuals. See also John Piper, "The Missionary Challenge in Paul's Life," <http:// www.desiringgod.org/library/sermons/85/ 110785.html>, site editor, Desiring God Ministries, November 7, 1985, accessed on 18 May 2004. See also John Piper, "'I Will Build My Church'—From All Peoples," <http://www.desiringgod.org/library/sermons/01/102801.html>, site editor, Desiring God Ministries, October 28, 2001, accessed on 18 May 2004

5   Piper, "Everlasting Truth for the Joy of All Peoples."

6   John Piper, "Surely He Has Borne Our Griefs," <http://www.desiring-god.org/library/sermons/93/031493.html>, site editor, Desiring God Ministries, March 14, 1993, accessed on 18 May 2004.

7   John Piper, "The Lord Is Great and Does Wondrous Things," <http:// www.desiringgod.org/library/sermons/91/042891.html>, site editor, Desiring God Ministries, April 28, 1991, accessed on 18 May 2004.

unreached peoples will not only be heard, but received.[8] Piper believes these promises are at the verge of being fulfilled because for the first time in history, unreached peoples are the focus of missionaries' attention.[9]

In the third set of passages, the psalmist prays with certainty that salvation will reach all people groups. Psalm 72 states that all nations will serve God and be blessed by him. Psalm 67 expresses confidence in God's sovereignty, all nations will receive salvation, and explains that God blesses his people so they may be a blessing to the nations.[10] Piper states that God's purpose for all the people groups is that he be known, praised, enjoyed, and feared. God desires that the nations know that he alone is God; and that he is righteous, sovereign, powerful, and gracious to those who believe in him.[11]

In the fourth set of passages, the psalmist expresses his desire to participate in making God's name recognized among all people groups. Psalm 18:49 states that David praises God among the nations. Psalm 87:9 and 108:3 state that David thanks God and sings praises to his name among the nations. Piper comments that Ps 57:8–9 demonstrates worship arises from a desire to exalt and magnify God among the nations so they may praise him.[12]

In addition to passages in Psalms and Isaiah, Gen 12:1–3 is a significant Old Testament Great Commission passage that emphasizes people groups as a priority in missions (seen also in Gen 18:18, 22:18, 26:4, and 28:14). Genesis 12:1-3 states that God

---

8   John Piper, "The Great Invitation: Call Others Too!," <http://www.desiringgod.org/library/sermons/88/080788.html>, site editor, Desiring God Ministries, August 7,1988, accessed on 18 May 2004.

9   Ibid.

10   Piper, "Let the Nations Be Glad!"

11   John Piper, "Let All the Peoples Praise Thee," <http://www.desiringgod.org/ library/sermons/86/110986.html>, site editor, Desiring God Ministries, November 9, 1986, accessed on 19 May 2004.

12   John Piper, "I Will Sing Praises to You Among the Nations," <http://www.desiringgod.org/library/sermons/91/062391.html>, site editor, Desiring God Ministries, June 23, 1991, accessed on 19 May 2004.

promises to bless all the families of the earth "All the families" designates a group smaller than a tribe, and similar to a clan.[13]

New Testament

Piper maintains Great Commission passages such as Luke 24:45–47, Acts 1:8, and Matt 28:18–20 all demonstrate Christ's understanding that the goal of missions is centered on reaching people groups rather than individuals. Luke 24:45–47 indicates that Christ's command to reach the people groups is found in the Old Testament.[14] Acts 1:8 suggests that the task of missions is for Christians to proclaim the gospel to the entire world, even to unreached peoples.[15]

In Matt 28:18–20, Piper sees the Great Commission's command to make disciples of "all the nations," *panta ta ethné*, as a reference to all people groups, not individuals or geographic countries/locations.[16] He explains the singular *ethnos* always refers to a

---

13   Piper, *Let the Nations Be Glad!*, 167–70.

14   Ibid., 185 n 25. Piper cites several passages in the Greek Old Testament that use the phrase, *panta ta ethnè*, to refer to missions including: Gen 18:8, 22:18, 26:4 Ps 48:2, 71:11, 81:8, 116:1; Isa 2:2, 25:7, 52:10, 56:7, 61:11, and 66:18–20.

15   John Piper, "The Spirit Wants the World for Christ," <http://www.desiringgod.org/library/sermons/84/060384.html>, site editor, Desiring God Ministries, June 6, 1984, accessed on 27 May 2004, John Piper, "The Price and the Preciousness of Spiritual Power," <http://www.desiringgod.org/library/sermons/91/022491.html>, site editor, Desiring God Ministries, February 24, 1991, accessed on 27 May 2004; John Piper, "Old and Young Shall Dream Together," <http://www.desiringgod.org/library/sermons/89/ 091089.html>, site editor, Desiring God Ministries, September 10, 1989, accessed on 27 May 2004; and John Piper, "That All the Nations Might Hear," <http://www.desiring god.org/library/sermons/00/102900.html>, site editor, Desiring God Ministries, October 29, 2000, accessed on 27 May 2004.

16   Piper, *Let the Nations Be Glad!*, 160. Piper believes the Great Commission's command to make disciples of all nations is valid for today. Since the promise, "I am with you always, to the end of the age," extends to the second coming of Christ, he reasons, the "you" cannot only refer to

people group or nation, and, while the plural *ethné* (and its variants) may mean Gentile individuals, it usually refers to a people group.[17] Additionally, of the nearly hundred times the Greek Old Testament uses the term (or its variants), almost every time it designates people groups other than Israel.[18]

Piper believes the apostle Paul also understood that the Great Commission's focus was on people groups. He states that when Paul examined Gen 17:4–5 (the promise that Abraham will be a father of a "multitude of nations"), Paul saw nations as people groups not related to Israel. Romans 4:11 explains that God justified Abraham by faith before circumcision, which demonstrates that people from all people groups who place their faith in Christ are heirs of Abraham and are included in his blessing (Gen 12:1–3).[19] Romans 4:16–17 confirms that Abraham is a father to people groups who place their faith in Christ.[20] Paul's understanding of the Great Commission's focus on people groups is also seen in Rom 15 where Paul quotes Old Testament passages that relate to peoples: Ps 18:49 (Rom 15:9); Deut 32:43 (Rom 15:10);

---

the apostles or those living during the time of Christ, but must include the generation living at the consummation of history.

17   Ibid., 161–67. Piper states in *panta ta ethnès* eighteen uses in the New Testament, the plural *ethnè* (or its variants) means Gentile individuals once (Matt 25:32); either Gentile individuals or people groups eight times (Matt 24:9, 24:14, 28:19, Luke 12:30, 24:47, Acts 14:16, Rom 1:5, and 2 Tim 4:17, 15:17); people groups three times based on context (Acts 2:5, 10:35, 17:26); and people groups six times based on the Old Testament (Mark 11:17, Luke 2:24, Acts 15:17, Gal 3:8, Rev 12:5, 15:4).

18   Ibid., 187

19   Ibid., 176; and John Piper, "Why Does It Matter Which Came First: Circumcision or Justification?," <http://www.desiringgod.org/library/sermons/99/082299.html>, site editor, Desiring God Ministries, August 22, 1999, accessed on 18 May 2004.

20   Piper, *Let the Nations Be Glad!*, 176–77; and John Piper, "The Faith–Grace–Certainty Connection," <http://www.desiringgod.org/library/sermons/99/091999.html>, site editor, Desiring God Ministries, September 19, 1999, accessed on 18 May 2004.

Ps 117:1 (Rom 15:11); and Isa 11:10 (Rom 15:12).[21] Later in Rom 15:18–24, Paul emphasizes the need for frontier missions. He states that he has completely proclaimed the gospel from Jerusalem to Illyricum, but realizes that evangelism is still needed in areas where missions work is complete.[22] His desire was to reach unreached peoples.

Piper believes the apostle John also understood that the Great Commission's focus was on people groups rather than individuals. Revelation 5:9 and John 11:52 state that Christ purchased from every tribe, language, people, and nation those who will be his children.[23] Other passages in Revelation depict the goal of missions as reaching all people groups for Christ: Rev 7:9–10, 14:6–7, 15:4, and 21:3.[24] Revelation 21:3 is especially important because it states there will be *peoples* not people in heaven,[25] indicating a diversity and multiplicity of ethnic groups. John 17:20 states that God uses the preaching of the word to bring people groups to himself.[26]

Piper's interpretation of *panta ta ethné* as people groups is essential to his missiology. He summarizes his position in ten statements.

---

21   Piper, *Let the Nations Be Glad!*, 178.

22   Piper, "The Revelation of God's Righteousness Where There Is No Church;" and Piper, "The Missionary Challenge of Paul's Life."

23   John Piper, "God Pursuit of Racial Diversity At Infinite Cost," <http://www.desiringgod.org/library/sermons/01/011401.html>, site editor, Desiring God Ministries, January 14, 2001, accessed on 26 May 2004; and John Piper, "I Have Other Sheep That Are Not of This Fold," <http://www.desiringgod.org/ library/sermons/85/111085/.html>, site editor, Desiring God Ministries, November 10, 1985, accessed on May 26, 2004.

24   Piper, *Let the Nations Be Glad!*, 183–84.

25   Ibid., 184 n 24. Piper notes that scholars from the United Bible Societies Greek New Testament and the Nestle-Aland Greek New Testament believe the word *laoi*, peoples, rather than *laos*, people, is the correct and earliest rendering of the term.

26   Piper, "Those Whom He Predestined He Also Called;" and Piper, *Desiring God*, 237.

1. The term *ethnos* in the New Testament never depicts Gentile individuals.
2. Usually, the term *ethné* can mean either Gentile individuals or people groups in the New Testament.
3. Only once in the New Testament does *panta ta ethné* mean Gentile individuals, nine times it means people groups, and eight times the meaning is unclear.
4. Almost every time the Greek Old Testament uses *panta ta ethné* it means nations outside Israel.
5. The promise God gave Abraham in Gen 12:1–3 (and other places) is cited in the New Testament and gives the mission of the church a people group focus.
6. The Old Testament shows how God's glory is manifested to all people groups.
7. Paul relates his understanding of missions back to the Old Testament promises concerning people groups.
8. The apostle John sees the goal of missions as gathering the elect from all people groups.
9. Based on the Old Testament, Luke 24:46–47 demonstrates that *panta ta ethné* indicates people groups.
10. Mark 11:17 explains that Christ may think about people groups when thinking about God's purpose for the world.[27]

SUFFERING AND MISSIONS

While Piper understands the goal of missions is to reach all people groups for Christ, he also understands that missionaries pay for their dedication. He quotes Dietrich Bonhoeffer's famous statement about the call to salvation and suffering: "When Christ calls a man, he bids him to come and die."[28] For the first three hundred years of Christianity's history, suffering, persecution, and

---

27 Piper, *Let the Nations Be Glad!*, 187.
28 Dietrich Bonhoeffer, *The Cost of Discipleship* (New York: Macmillan, 1963), 99; quoted in Piper, *Let the Nations Be Glad!*, 74.

death were not uncommon.[29] According to Piper, Raymond Lull in the early fourteenth century, at seventy-nine years old, went back on the mission field in northern Africa and became a martyr.[30] Authorities imprisoned John Bunyan, author of *Pilgrim's Progress*, for twelve years for preaching the gospel.[31] Authorities also imprisoned Hristo Kulichev, a Congregational pastor in Bulgaria during the Cold War for preaching.[32] Non-Christians are persecuting millions of Christians today for their faith.[33] David Barrett estimates that in 2002, 165,000 Christians died for their faith and by 2025, 210,000 Christians will be martyred yearly.[34] Around 45.4 million Christians have been martyred in the 1900s;

---

29   John Piper, "The Noble Army of the Martyrs Praise Thee," <http://www.desiringgod.org/library/sermons/93/052393.html>, site editor, Desiring God Ministries, May 23, 1993, accessed on 1 June 2004. See also J. Herbert Kane, *A Concise History of the Christian World: A Panoramic View of Missions from Pentecost to the Present*, rev. ed. (Grand Rapids: Baker, 1982), 29–33; and Ruth A. Tucker, *From Jerusalem to Irian Jaya: A Biographical History of Christian Missions* (Grand Rapids: Academie, 1983), 25–42.

30   John Piper, "Closed Countries and Retirement," <http://www.desiringgod.org/library/topics/missions/retirement.html>, site editor, Desiring God Ministries, October 8, 1988, accessed on 2 June 2004. Tucker, *From Jerusalem to Irian Jaya*, 52–56, provides a summary of the life of Lull.

31   John Piper, "Luther, Bunyan, Bible and Pain," <http://www.desiringgod.org/library/fresh_words/1999/011999.html>, site editor, Desiring God Ministries, January 19, 1999, accessed on 2 June 2004. See also John Piper, *The Smile of God: The Fruit of Affliction in the Lives of John Bunyan, William Cowper, and David Brainerd* (Wheaton: Crossway, 2001), 41–81.

32   John Piper, "Spreading Spiritual Power through Persecution," <http://www.desiringgod.org/library/sermons/91/050591.html>, site editor, Desiring God Ministries, May 5, 1991, accessed on 2 June 2004.

33   John Piper, "Blessed Are the Persecuted," <http://www.desiringgod.org/library/sermons/86/031686.html>, site editor, Desiring God Ministries, March 16, 1986, accessed on 2 June 2004.

34   David Barrett, "Annual Statistical Table on Global Mission: 2002," *International Bulletin of Missionary Research* 26, no. 1 (January 2002): 23; quoted in Piper, *Let the Nations Be Glad!*, 75.

70 million have been killed since Christianity's inception.[35] Piper states, "The Great Commission will not be completed without suffering;"[36] . . . "martyrdom is normal Christianity."[37]

Piper explains not only is suffering a part of missions, but also God wills the missionary (and the Christian in general) to suffer (1 Thess 3:3). First Peter 4:1 and John 15:20 state that as God appointed the persecution and death of Christ, God appoints suffering for the Christian.[38] Hebrews 13:12–14 explains Christ suffered for the nations. He relinquished the comfort of heaven for the need of the world.[39] One missionary connects Christ's suffering with the Christian's when he gives his reaction to a graveyard in Miango, Nigeria where thirty-three of the fifty-six graves are children of missionary families: "The only way we can understand the graveyard at Miango is to remember that God also buried his Son on the mission field."[40]

---

35   David Barrett, George T. Kuruan, and Todd M. Johnson, *World Christian Encyclopedia: A Comparative Study of Churches and Religions—AD 30 to 2000*, vol 1 (Oxford: Oxford University Press, 2001) 11; quoted in Piper, *Let the Nations Be Glad!*, 75, 75 n 4.

36   John Piper, "Arming Yourself with the Purpose to Suffer," <http://www. desiringgod.org/library/sermons/94/100294.html>, site editor, Desiring God Ministries, October 2, 1994, accessed on 1 June 2004.

37   John Piper, "Nothing Can Separate Us from the Love of Christ," <http:// www.desiringgod.org/library/sermons/02/090802.html>, site editor, Desiring God Ministries, September 8, 2002, accessed on 2 June 2004.

38   Piper, "Arming Yourself with the Purpose to Suffer;" John Piper, "Suffering for the Sake of the Body," <http://www.desiringgod.org/library/tbi/ suffering.html>, site editor, Desiring God Ministries, accessed on 1 June 2004; and John Piper, "To Live Upon God that is Invisible: Suffering and Service in the Life of John Bunyan," <http://www. desiringgod.org/ library/biographies/99bunyan.html>, site editor, Desiring God Ministries, February 2, 1999, accessed on 1 June 2004. Piper, "Is God Less Glorious Because He Ordained that Evil Be," provides an explanation of the wider subject of God's will and evil.

39   John Piper, "Let Us Go with Jesus, Bearing Reproach," <http://www. desiringgod.org/library/sermons/97/092797.html>, site editor, Desiring God Ministries, September, 1997, accessed on 1 June 2004.

40   Piper, "Called to Rejoice in Suffering: For Holiness and Hope."

Piper gives six reasons why God wills the missionary to suffer: 1) to increase faith; 2) to increase reward in heaven; 3) to make others courageous; 4) to "fill up" what was "lacking" in Christ's afflictions; 5) to encourage the missionary to go; and 6) to manifest Christ.[41] Suffering increases a missionary's faith by removing pride and trust in others and causing him to rely[42] and place hope in God.[43] Piper quotes Paton, who barely escaped martyrdom, as an example. Paton, while hiding from his persecutors, stated, "Never, in all my sorrows, did my Lord draw nearer to me, and speak more soothingly in my soul, than when the moonlight flickered among these chestnut leaves, and the night air played on my throbbing brow, as I told all my heart to Jesus."[44]

Suffering increases a missionary's reward in heaven. Second Corinthians 4:17 links suffering with ability to enjoy God. Piper states there is a "causal connection" between how a Christian responds to suffering on earth and how he is capable of enjoying and savoring the glory of God in heaven.[45] Suffering prepares the Christian for glory and should motivate him to persevere during

---

41   Piper, *Let the Nations Be Glad!*, 86–102.

42   John Piper, "Children, Heirs, Fellow Sufferers," <http://www.desiring-god. org/library/sermons/02/042102.html>, site editor, Desiring God Ministries, April 21, 2002, accessed on 1 June 2004 and John Piper, "Fathers Who Give Hope," <http://www. desiringgod.org/library/sermons/86/061586.html>, site editor, Desiring God Ministries, June 15, 1986, accessed on 1 June 2004.

43   John Piper, "We Rejoice in Our Tribulations," <http://www.desiringgod. org/library/sermons/99/111499.html>, site editor, Desiring God Ministries, November 14, 1999, accessed on 1 June 2004; and John Piper, "The Love of God Has Been Poured Out Within Our Hearts," <http:// www.desiringgod.org/library/sermons/99/ 112899.html>, site editor, Desiring God Ministries, November 28, 1999, accessed on 1 June 2004.

44   John Paton, in John Piper, *You Will Be Eaten by Cannibals! Courage in the Cause of World Missions. Lessons in the Life of John G. Paton*, audio cd (Minneapolis: Desiring God Ministries, 2000).

45   John Piper, "Called to Suffer and Rejoice: For an Eternal Weight of Glory," <http://www.desiringgod.org/library/sermons/92/090692.html>, site editor, Desiring God Ministries, September 6, 1992, accessed on 2 June 2004

times of trial.[46] In discussing Rom 8:14–18, Piper states the connection another way: "No pain, no gain. No cross, no crown. No suffering, no inheritance. That's the way it is."[47] If God gives the same reward in heaven (the enjoyment of God) to all in the same amount, then stating the Christian should rejoice in suffering makes no sense.[48]

A missionary's suffering makes others fearless. Philippians 1:14 states that suffering makes Christians bold for the gospel.[49] Martyrdom encourages Christians because it makes them focus on eternity.[50] Piper gives the example of Chet Bitterman, a Wycliffe missionary murdered in Columbia. After his execution, applications to the organization doubled. While the impact of the murders of Jim Elliot, Nate Saint, Ed McCully, Pete Fleming, and Roger Youderian by the Huaorani (Auca) may never be known,[51] the fact the organization increased tremendously soon after their execution indicates a boldness not seen before. Piper cites church fathers Tertullian and Jerome who state that the blood of martyrs establishes the Church.[52]

A missionary's suffering completes what is "lacking" in Christ's afflictions. Piper is not stating Christ's afflictions are insufficient. As stated in chapter 2, Piper uses Col 1:24–29 to indicate that Christ's afflictions lack an evangelistic witness to all the nations.

---

46   John Piper, "Calling All Clay Pots: A Celebration of Ministry," <http:// www. desiringgod.org/library/sermons/82/091282.html>, site editor, Desiring God Ministries, September 12, 1982, accessed on 2 June 2004.

47   John Piper, "Children, Heirs, Fellow Sufferers."

48   Piper, "Blessed Are the Persecuted;" and Piper, *Let the Nations Be Glad!*, 88

49   John Piper, "Christian Courage," <http://www.desiringgod.org/library/ fresh_words/1999/051199.html>, site editor, Desiring God Ministries, May 11, 1999, 2002, accessed on 2 June 2004.

50   John Piper, "Execution, Escape, and Eaten By Worms: How the Word of God Grew," <http://www.desiringgod.org/library/sermons/91/120191. html>, site editor, Desiring God Ministries, December 1, 1991, accessed on 2 June 2004.

51   Piper, *Let the Nations Be Glad!*, 90–91.

52   Piper, "Execution, Escape, and Eaten By Worms."

First Thessalonians 1:5–6 and 2 Cor 1:5-6 indicate a similar idea: God uses the suffering of the Christian to proclaim the gospel.[53] Piper recounts a story of a converted African warrior who repeatedly went to a village to share the gospel. Three times the villagers beat him almost to death, but after the third beating, the village came to Christ.[54]

Suffering in missions prompts the spread of the gospel. Acts 8:1 and 11:19 indicate that because of persecution the early church spread the faith to Judea, Samaria, and to other people groups.[55] Piper believes persecution led whole Uzbek towns to come to Christ in the 1900s. Koreans who fled to the Soviet Union were moved by Joseph Stalin to Tashkent. The Korean Christians witnessed to the Uzbeks and within two generations, villages came to Christ.[56] Luke 21:12–13 states that Christians should expect to be taken before the government and imprisoned in order that they may proclaim the gospel.[57] Piper recounts the story of a Mozambique evangelist whom authorities imprisoned for sharing his faith. In jail, he met the chief of police and led him to Christ. Af-

---

53   John Piper, "Suffering for the Sake of the Body: The Pursuit of People Through Pain ," <http://www.desiringgod.org/library/tbi/suffering. html>, site editor, Desiring God Ministries, accessed on 2 June 2004; and John Piper, " Brothers, Our Affliction IS For Their Comfort," <http://www.desiringgod.org/library/topics/leadership/brothers_afflict/ html>, site editor, Desiring God Ministries, accessed on 2 June 2004.

54   Michael Card, "Wounded in the House of Friends," Virtue (March/April 1991): 28–29, 69; quoted in Piper, Let the Nations Be Glad!, 93–94.

55   John Piper, "He Saw the Grace of God and Was Glad," <http://www. desiringgod.org/ library/sermons/91/112491.html>, site editor, Desiring God Ministries, November 24, 1991 accessed on 3 June 2004; and Piper, "Spreading Spiritual Power through Persecution."

56   Piper, "He Saw the Grace of God and Was Glad;" and Piper, Let the Nations Be Glad!, 95–96.

57   John Piper, "Risk and the Cause of God," <http://www.desiringgod.org/ library/ sermons/87/050387.html>, site editor, Desiring God Ministries, November 24, 1991 accessed on 3 June 2004; and John Piper, "Christ's Purposes in Evangelism," <http:// www.desiringgod.org/library/sermons/88/052288.html>, site editor, Desiring God Ministries, May 5, 1988, accessed on 3 June 2004.

ter his conversion, the police chief gave the evangelist permission to share Christ throughout his area of control.[58]

A missionary's suffering manifests Christ. Philippians 3:7–8 states that knowing Christ surpasses all sufferings and losses.[59] Second Corinthians 12:9–10 explains that a Christian's weakness magnifies the power of Christ by giving him the ability to endure.[60] Suffering, happily received, demonstrates the value Christian place on God.[61]

---

58 Piper, *Let the Nations Be Glad!*, 97–98.

59 John Piper, "Called to Suffer and Rejoice: That We Might Gain Christ," <http://www.desiringgod.org/library/sermons/92/082392.html>, site editor, Desiring God Ministries, August 23, 1992, accessed on 3 June 2004; and John Piper, "Going Hard After a Holy God," <http://www.desiringgod.org/library/sermons/92/082392.html>, site editor, Desiring God Ministries, January 8, 1984, accessed on 3 June 2004.

60 John Piper, "Christ's Power Is Made Perfect in Weakness," <http://www.desiring god.org/library/sermons/91/071491.html>, site editor, Desiring God Ministries, July 14, 1991, accessed on 3 June 2004.

61 Piper, *Let the Nations Be Glad!*, 99, 100.

7

PIPER'S UNDERSTANDING OF MISSIONS COMPARED WITH DAVID BOSCH AND DONALD MCGAVRAN

WHY BOSCH AND MCGAVRAN?

David Bosch (1929–1992) and Donald McGavran (1897-1990) were two eminent missiologists that left a profound mark on cross-cultural evangelism. Both are respected for their work in evangelical/conservative and ecumenical/liberal fields. Works have been dedicated to them or written about them.[1] Bosch, influenced by Barthian Calvinism, represents a neo-orthodox, ecumenical strand of missiology. A former missionary and head of the department of missiology at the University of South Africa until his untimely death, he focused on providing a biblical foundation for mission, distinguishing mission from evangelism, understanding the meaning of the gospel in Africa, and bridging the gulf between evangelicals and ecumenicals.[2] One of his books, *Transforming Mission*, still over thirty years later, is one of the most recognized missiology texts today. McGavran, influenced by Arminianism in the Disciples of Christ, a small denomination in the United States,

---

1   For Bosch, see J. J. Kritzinger and W. A. Saayman, eds. *Mission in Creative Tension: A Dialogue with David Bosch* (Pretoria, South Africa: South African Missiological Society, 1990), 196; Willem Saayman and Klippies Kritzinger, eds., *Mission in Bold Humility: David Bosch's Works Considered* (Maryknoll, NY: Orbis, 1996). For McGavran see: A. R. Tippett, ed., *God, Man and Church Growth* (Grand Rapids: Eerdmans, 1973).

2   J. Kevin Livingston, "The Legacy of David J. Bosch," *International Bulletin of Missionary Research 23*, no 1 (January 1999): 28–29.

represents an evangelical strand of missiology common in North America. A former missionary and professor of mission, church growth, and South Asian studies at the School of World Mission at Fuller Theological Seminary, he is considered to be the father of the Church Growth Movement.[3] His works helped transform the focus of evangelical missions from geographic nations to people groups.[4] In comparing them with Piper, we will see where Piper fits within the broader field of missiology.

Bosch's Understanding of Missiology Compared to Piper[5]

Definition of Terms

Bosch and Piper use the terms "mission" and "missions" to describe their understanding of missiology. While Piper rarely distinguishes between the words and mostly uses the term "missions," Bosch separates the words and mostly uses the term "mission." Bosch defines mission as: "the total task which God has set the Church for the salvation of the world. It is the task of the Church in movement, the Church that lives for others, the Church that is not only concerned about herself, that turns herself 'inside out' (Hoekendijk) toward the world"[6] that includes the "redemption of the universe and the glorification of God."[7]

3　　Donald McGavran, *The Bridges of God: A Study in the Strategies of Missions*, rev. ed. (New York: Friendship, 1955), front cover.

4　　Ralph D.Winter, "Four Men, Three Eras, Two Transitions: Modern Missions," 41–42, in Ralph D. Winter and Steven C. Hawthorne, eds. *Perspectives on the World Christian Movement: A Reader*, rev. ed. (Pasadena: William Carey Library, 1992).

5　　John Kevin Livingston, "A Missiology of the Road: The Theology of Mission and Evangelism in the Writings of David J. Bosch" (Ph.D. diss., University of Aberdeen, 1989), provides a solid summary of Bosch's position.

6　　David Bosch, *Witness to the World: The Christian Mission in Theological Perspective* (Atlanta: John Knox, 1980), 17, 18.

7　　David Bosch, "Evangelism: Theological Currents and Cross-currents Today," *International Bulletin of Missionary Research* 11, no. 3 (July 1987): 100.

Bosch realizes there is confusion between the terms "mission" and "missions."[1] He distinguishes mission from missions by using the terms *missio Dei*, the mission of God, and *missiones ecclesiae*, the missionary enterprise of the Church, respectively.[2] He states mission as *missio Dei* is "God's self revelation as the One who loves the world, God's involvement in and with the world, the nature and activity of God, which embraces the church and the world, and in which the church is privileged to participate."[3] *Missiones ecclesiae* are the actual work done by the Church that correspond to the *missio Dei*.[4] Accordingly, missions as mission is wider in scope than church planting or evangelism.[5] Because Piper mostly uses missions and Bosch mostly uses mission to describe similar ideas, these words will be used in comparing and contrasting their thoughts.

Bosch and Piper both believe there is a connection between mission(s) and evangelism. They disagree on how they are associated.[6] Bosch maintains mission and evangelism must be held together in "creative tension."[7] Mission is more encompassing than evangelism. Mission should not be separated from evangelism. Mission is not proclaiming the gospel internationally and

---

1   David Bosch, "The Quest for Mission Today," *Journal of Theology for South Africa* 1 (December 1972): 5 n *. David Bosch, *Transforming Mission: Paradigm Shifts in the Theology of Mission* (Marknoll, NY: Orbis, 1991), 8–11, provides thirteen characteristics of mission: Christianity is missionary; missiology is part of theology; mission cannot be defined; mission portrays a relationship between God and the world; mission is done in with tension between God and man; the church is missionary; foreign missions and home missions are not separate; there is a difference between the mission and missions; there should be no separation between the spiritual and social aspect of man in mission; mission is God's yes to the world; mission is God's no to the world; evangelism must be included in mission; and mission is a type of sacrament.

2   Bosch, *Transforming Mission*, 10.

3   Ibid.

4   Bosch, "The Quest for Mission Today," 5 n *.

5   Bosch, *Transforming Mission*, 391.

6   Bosch, *Witness to the World*, 20.

7   Ibid., 15, 221; and Bosch, *Transforming Mission*, 8–11.

evangelism is not witnessing nationally.[8] Mission is "evangelism plus social action,"[9] Mission promotes causes that fight against exploitation, discrimination, and violence as well as promoting salvation, healing, and liberation.[10] Evangelism involves the proclamation of the gospel in all cultures. Evangelism, however, is not just "winning souls for Jesus." Evangelism is "calling people to mission,"[11] and includes bringing a nonbeliever to church; telling the non-believer about God's actions in history and the future; inviting, not manipulating, the person to come to Christ; living a lifestyle that promotes the gospel; taking chances in the witness encounter that involves the possibility of a change of heart in both the evangelist and lost person; and explaining to the non-believer that the gift of salvation is not about temporal or earthly happiness, but eternity.[12]

Bosch's Foundation, Motivation, Goal for Mission

Bosch, like Piper, recognizes the glory of God is important to mission. Bosch states that God's revelation of his glory is one of two attributes in mission (the other attribute is human responsibility). God's glory emphasizes God's sovereignty in mission. God's initiative is seen in his interaction with believers in the Old and New Testament. In the Old Testament God uses Israel to witness

---

8   Bosch, *Witness to the World*, 20 and Bosch, *Transforming Mission*, 9-10.

9   Bosch, *Witness to the World*, 16–17; Bosch, "Evangelism and Mission: The Current Debate," 10–11, 18; and Bosch, "In Search of a New Evangelical Understanding," in Bruce Nicholls, ed., *In Word and Deed: Evangelism and Social Responsibility* (Grand Rapids: Eerdmans, 1985), 81.

10   David Bosch, "Mission—An Attempt at a Definition," *Church Sense* (April 25, 1986): 11. See also David Bosch, "Evangelism: Theological Currents and Cross-currents Today," *International Bulletin of Missionary Research 11*, no. 3 (July 1987): 100.

11   Bosch, "Evangelism: A Holistic Approach," 59.

12   Bosch, "Evangelism: Theological Currents and Cross-currents Today," 100.

to the nations. In the New Testament God uses the Holy Spirit in the lives of his children to accomplish his purpose.[13]

Since Bosch sees mission as *missio Dei*, he believes the foundation, motive, aim of mission is more extensive than God's glory. Mission must include transformation as well as evangelization.[14] Bosch, therefore, holds a position contrary to Piper's understanding of the goal of missions, especially Piper's interpretation of *panta ta ethné* as people groups. Bosch realizes evangelism is the heart of mission[15] and the gospel must be contextualized into every culture, but he believes exegesis of *panta ta ethné* demonstrates that the term does not mean ethno-linguistic peoples.[16] He states that Matthew used the term more broadly to explain that Christ is the savior of all humankind.[17] He maintains that *ethné* in the LXX, and its equivalent in the Hebrew Old Testament, *gôyim*, is the "religioethical" classification "Gentiles and pagans," not homogeneous people groups. In the New Testament, *ethné* depicts salvation history and shows a universal covenant and, therefore, does not require that interpretation.[18] He also believes exegetes have read a modern problem back into the text and states the Great Commission "can therefore not . . . imply that the Christian mission is to be carried out 'people to people,' but that it is to reach far beyond the confines that existed up to that time."[19]

Bosch believes transformation in mission must emulate Jesus' ministry and focus, which includes not only evangelism, but also liberation and healing. He believes these three areas of Christ's

---

13   David Bosch, "Reflections on Biblical Models of Mission," in James M. Phillips and Robert T. Coote, eds., *Toward the 21st Century in Christian Mission* (Grand Rapids: Eerdamans, 1993), 184–85.

14   Bosch, *Witness to the World*, 244.

15   Bosch, *Transforming Mission*, 10.

16   David Bosch, "The Structure of Mission: An Exposition of Matthew 28:16–20," in Wilbert R. Shenk, ed., *Exploring Church Growth* (Grand Rapids: Eerdmans, 1983), 236.

17   Bosch, *Transforming Mission*, 63.

18   Bosch, "The Structure of Mission," 235–36.

19   Ibid., 235.

ministry cannot be isolated from one another. Their connected-ness is seen especially in Luke.[20] When Luke discusses the healing ministry of Christ, he associates it with liberation and salvation. He expanded healing to include faith, salvation, and forgiveness as well as physical healing. Faith produced by healing leads to sal-vation, "spiritual healing," as when Christ saved those whom evil spirits possessed and the physically ill (Luke 8:1–2).[21] Healing also leads to forgiveness of sins as when Christ heals the paralytic (Luke 5:17–26).[22]

When Luke discusses liberation, he focuses on people de-spised by his audience.[23] He shows how Christ calls them to repen-tance and faith,[24] and in the process, tries to dismantle prejudice against them. Christ "empowers" them by replacing prejudice, suffering, and abuse (negative lowliness) with selflessness, service, and meekness, (positive lowliness). Empowerment is salvation.[25] Luke's commission in Luke 4:16–21 focuses on all these areas and has supplanted Matthew's commission in Matt 28:16–20 as the "Great Commission" in some theological fields.[26]

Bosch's Understanding of the Need for Mission

While Piper discusses hell, Bosch rarely mentions it. When Bosch does, he states that conversion to Christ for fear of hell is an improper motivation.[27] He also states that salvation is freedom

---

20   David Bosch, "Mission in Jesus' Way: A Perspective from Luke's Gospel," *Missionalia* 17 (April 1989): 4–5. See also Bosch, *Transforming Mission*, 84–122.

21   Neal Flanagan, "The What and How of Salvation in Luke-Acts," in D. Durken, ed., *Sin, Salvation and the Spirit* (Collegeville: Liturgical Press, 1979), 211; in Bosch, "Mission in Jesus' Way," 11.

22   Bosch, "Mission in Jesus' Way," 11.

23   These people include: Samaritans (Luke 9:51–56, 10:6, 10:30–37), women (Luke 8:1–3), tax-collectors (Luke 3:12, 5:27–32, 18:9–30), and the poor (Luke 4:16–30, 16:19–31).

24   Bosch, "Mission in Jesus' Way," 14–15.

25   Ibid., 8.

26   Bosch, *Transforming Mission*, 84.

27   David Bosch, "The Church in Dialogue: From Self-delusion to Vulnera-

from "eternal judgment,"[28] implying that hell is eternal in some sense. He does not elaborate on whether he believes hell is torment for eternity or annihilation.

Bosch differs with Piper regarding the atonement and the necessity of placing conscious faith in Christ. While Piper is certain only personal faith in Christ provides salvation, Bosch is unsure. Bosch states that other religions are genuine and must be respected,[29] but Christians still can confront other religions' followers with the gospel.[30] He indicates that there may be other means to salvation besides conscious faith in Christ. Non-Christians should be able to think as they desire, and Christians should treat non-Christians' religions as sacrosanct.[31] Bosch is uncomfortable with "sterile," absolutist positions and argues for a "creative tension" between exclusivism and pluralism.[32]

Gerald H. Anderson comments that the World Council of Churches' World Conference on Mission and Evangelism in San Antonio best summarizes Bosch's position on salvation: "We cannot point to any other way of salvation than Jesus Christ; at the same time we cannot set limits to the saving power of God."[33]

---

bility," *Missiology* 16 (April 1988): 144.

28 Bosch, *Witness to the World*, 218.

29 David Bosch, *Theology of Religions* (Pretoria, South Africa: University of South Africa, 1977), Study Guide 1 for MSA301-B, 166; quoted in J du Preez, "David Bosch's Theology of Religions: An Exercise in Humility," Kritzinger and Saayman, *Mission in Creative Tension: A Dialogue with David Bosch*, 196.

30 David Bosch, "Vision for Mission," *International Review of Mission* 76, no. 301 (January 1987): 12.

31 Bosch, "The Church in Dialogue," 136–37.

32 Bosch, *Transforming Mission*, 483.

33 Commission on World Mission and Evangelism, "San Antonio: Report, Section One," *International Review of Mission* 78, nos. 311–12 (1989): 345–56; in Gerald H. Anderson, "Theology of Religions: The Epitome of Mission Theology," in Willem Saayman and Klippies Kritzinger, eds., *Mission in Bold Humility: David Bosch's Works Considered* (Maryknoll, NY: Orbis, 1996), 119. Anderson explains Bosch played a major role in drafting the statement.

Instead of focusing on hell and the fate of people in other religions, Bosch spends a significant amount of time trying to resolve the theological differences between ecumenicals and evangelicals. He praises and criticizes both groups and has spoken at their conferences including Lausanne and Pattaya (evangelical) and Melbourne and San Antonio (ecumenical). In 1983, he helped write the World Evangelical Fellowship's position (evangelical) on the nature and mission of the church, and in 1987 he wrote the World Council of Churches' position (ecumenical) on evangelism.[34] He wrote in a *Festschrift* for Anderson (evangelical)[35] and, in a work dedicated to Bosch, people from both groups wrote on him.[36] In *Transforming Mission*, he seemed encouraged that branches of Christendom, evangelical, Catholic, Orthodox, and Protestant appear to be uniting and finding a balance between their areas of conflict.[37]

The Role of Suffering in Mission

Piper and Bosch believe suffering is necessary and essential to Christianity. Bosch believes the Greek term *marturía* connects suffering and mission.[38] Israel's exile in Babylon, the servant songs in Isaiah 53, and the mission theology of Paul in 2 Corinthians are examples.[39] Bosch explains that Israel became more powerful as she became less focused on mission. Only when God took her power did she became mission minded.[40] Isaiah 53 shows the Servant acts as a witness through patient suffering for others. Christ became the "true Missionary" through his suffering and death.[41]

---

34   Livingston, "The Legacy of David J. Bosch," 28–29.

35   Bosch, "Reflections on Biblical Models of Mission," 175–92, in Phillips and Coote, *Toward the 21st Century in Christian Mission*.

36   For example, evangelical missiologists Anderson and Shenk and ecumenical missiologists John S. Pobee and William R. Burrows wrote pieces in Saayman and Kritzinger, *Mission in Bold Humility*.

37   Bosch, *Transforming Mission*, 408.

38   Bosch, *Witness to the World*, 73.

39   Livingston, "A Missiology of the Road," 252–55.

40   Bosch, *Witness to the World*, 71–72.

41   David Bosch, "The Church Without Privileges," *Asfacts* 19 (September):

In Second Corinthians, Paul promotes suffering and weakness and rejects pride. Bosch comments that Paul's understanding of suffering in the church is the difference between mission and his opponents at Corinth.[42]

Bosch and Piper also agree that suffering centers on the cross of Christ.[43] Bosch states that suffering makes Christianity unique.[44] Like Piper, Bosch also quotes Bonhoeffer's famous statement:

> To endure the cross is not a tragedy; it is the suffering which is the fruit of an exclusive allegiance to Jesus Christ. When it comes it is not an accident. But a necessity . . . the cross is not the terrible end to an otherwise god-fearing and happy life, but it meets us at the beginning of our communion with Christ. When Christ calls a man, he bids him to come and die.[45]

Bosch and Piper differ on the focus and intent of suffering. Piper believes suffering is God-ordained, and in some sense, a privilege. Suffering for Christ, especially when proclaiming the gospel indicates a Christian's joy is in Christ. Bosch sees suffering as something potentially negative, as seen in his connection of suffering with oppression and prejudice. Those who suffer must be helped. The difference may lie in their foundation for mission. Piper centers on the glory of God, which encourages the priority of the proclamation of the gospel while Bosch focuses on the *missio Dei*, which encourages fellowship and service but dilutes

---

1977; quoted in Livingston, "A Missiology of the Road," 253.

42 David Bosch, "The Why and How of a True Biblical Foundation for Mission," in *Zending op Weg naar de toekomst. Opstles aangenboden ann Prof. Dr. J. Verkuyl* (Kampen: Kok, 1978), 43–44; quoted in Livingston, "A Missiology of the Road," 254.

43 David Bosch, "The Vulnerability of Mission," *Zeitschrift für Missionswissenschaft und Religionswissenschaft* 76, no. 3 (Jan 1992): 205. See also Piper, "Called to Suffer and Rejoice: To Finish the Aim of Christ's Afflictions."

44 Bosch, "The Vulnerability of Mission," 205–07.

45 Dietrich Bonhoeffer, *The Cost of Discipleship* (London: SCM, 1976), 78; quoted in Bosch, "The Vulnerability of Mission," 208.

focus on evangelism. Bosch states that the biblical idea of witness includes all three concepts.[46] Bosch believes that since people are suffering, the Christian must focus on serving them and helping liberate and heal them. Piper believes help must go deeper than physical and psychological needs and concentrate on the spiritual condition.

McGavran's Understanding of Missiology Compared to Piper

Definition and Explanation of Terms

McGavran and Piper differ in their use of the terms "missions" and "evangelism." While Piper believes that the terms are overlapping, but distinct, McGavran sees little difference between them. McGavran substitutes the term "effective evangelism" for evangelism and states that effective evangelism and missions are synonymous with church growth.[47] Similar to Piper, McGavran uses E-1, E-2, E-3 to distinguish types of effective evangelism/missions/church growth, but adds the designations E-0, E-1-A, E-1-B, E-1-C, and E-1-D for more detail.[48]

McGavran and Piper also differ in their use of the terms "people group" and "reached." Piper, whose approach is strictly biblical rather than missiological, believes the terms are ambiguous. On the other hand, McGavran maintains that both phrases can be defined and incorporates sociology into his definition. McGavran states that a "people" or "people group" is "a tribe or caste, a clan or lineage, or tightly knit segment of any society."[49] He states that "reached" refers to many members of a people coming to know Christ and being properly discipled. Unreached or hidden peoples are people groups who are prevented access to the gospel, or

46 Bosch, *Witness to the World*, 73, 227.

47 Donald McGavran, "My Pilgrimage in Mission," *International Bulletin of Missionary Research* 10, vol. 1 (January 1986): 57–58.

48 Donald McGavran, *Understanding Church Growth*, rev. ed. (Grand Rapids: Eerdmans, 1980), 71–72.

49 See also: McGavran, *The Bridges of God*, 13.

peoples who live among Christians but have a different language, race, or culture. His position is like Piper in that there are many peoples who have not been evangelized effectively but is different in defining a people as "reached."[50] Piper believes Scripture is purposely obtruse, and the Christian should be as well. Piper argues that if the Bible gave a definition of "reached," when Christians accomplish the task, they may stop sharing the gospel.[51]

McGavran's Motivation for Missions

McGavran's motivation for missions differs from Piper's. While McGavran sees the importance of the glory of God in missions,[52] he believes the motive for missions should be God's desire to see churches grow numerically.[53] A Christian must witness to the "winnable while they are winnable." He implies God cares more about peoples who are receptive to the gospel than about peoples who reject Christ.[54]

McGavran believes Scripture shows God searching for receptive people groups. In the Old Testament, God found Israel in Egypt and remained loyal to her. In the New Testament, God in Christ came to save "countable bodies" and commissioned churches to go to receptive cultures.[55] Matthew 9:37–38 calls the apostles to pray that God would send laborers to reap a bountiful harvest. The Great Commission in Matt 28:18–20 indicates that sharing

---

50   McGavran, *Understanding Church Growth*, 73–74.

51   Piper, *Let the Nations Be Glad!*, 192–95.

52   McGavran and Arn, How to Grow a Church, 6; Donald McGavran, "Presence and Proclamation in Christian Mission," in Donald Mc-Gavran, ed., *Eye of the Storm: The Great Debate in Mission* (Waco: Word, 1972), 216; McGavran, "Will Uppsala Betray the Two Billion?," in *Eye of the Storm*, 239; and McGavran, *Understanding Church Growth*, 190.

53   McGavran, Understanding Church Growth, 41; Donald McGavran, "The God Who Finds His Mission," *International Review of Mission* 51 (1962): 304; and McGavran, Critical Issues, 249–50.

54   Donald McGavran, ed., *Church Growth and Christian Mission* (New York: Harper & Row, 1965), 82.

55   McGavran, *Understanding Church Growth*, 35–38.

the gospel results in peoples being converted and discipled.[56] The woman who found the missing coin (Luke 15:8–10), the shepherd who found the absent sheep (Luke 15:1–8), and the master's compelling the poor to attend the great banquet (Luke 14:15–24) represent parables that demonstrate God wills to save the lost.[57]

McGavran's Understanding of the Need for Missions

McGavran's understanding of the need for missions is like Piper's. McGavran does not discuss hell, but he believes in the authority of Scripture.[58] His belief that Christ is the only way to salvation indicates that he sees only Christians in heaven. He states that believing in Christ makes an "eternal difference."[59] Elsewhere, he writes salvation comes through Christ alone,[60] and that Christ is the final authority,[61] and the "only savior."[62] Eternal damnation is not discussed.

McGavran's position on the fate of the unevangelized is not clear and he is unsure of their eternal destiny. Concerning their fate he states: "Should He [God] so choose he can bring those who know nothing of Jesus Christ back into fellowship with himself. But the means by which he might do this (and whether in point of fact he ever does do it) remains hidden. God has not chosen

---

56   Ibid., 32–40.

57   Ibid., 34–35.

58   Donald McGavran and Win C. Arn, *Ten Steps for Church Growth* (New York: Harper and Row, 1977), 24; *How to Grow a Church*, 6; Donald McGavran, *The Clash Between Christianity and Cultures* (Washington: Canon, 1974), 52; and Donald McGavran, ed., *Critical Issues in Missions Tomorrow* (Chicago: Moody, 1972), 194.

59   Donald McGavran, "Criticism of the Working Draft on Mission," in *Eye of the Storm*, 237; and Donald McGavran, "The Biblical Base from Which Adjustments are Made," in Tetsunao Yamamori and Charles R. Taber. eds., *Christopaganism or Indigenous Christianity* (South Pasadena, CA: William Cary Library, 1975), 35–55, esp. 37, 54, 55.

60   Ibid., 234; McGavran and Arn, *Ten Steps for Church Growth*, 28.

61   McGavran, *The Clash Between Christianity and Cultures*, 28.

62   Donald McGavran, "Essential Evangelism: An Open Letter to Dr. Hoekendijk," in *Eye of the Storm*, 56.

to reveal this in Scripture."[63] On this point, McGavran seems to agree more with Erickson than Piper.

Ancillary to McGavran's belief that missions needs to focus on sharing the gospel is his condemnation of missions centering on humanitarian aid/social action. However important, he believes the need in missions is not liberating the oppressed or opening schools, hospitals, and orphanages. When evangelism is not primary, these ministries handicap the church, institutionalize missions, hinder church growth, and contradict Scripture.[64] The only proper time to use humanitarian aid/social action is as a platform to proclaim the gospel in closed areas when there are no other means available. Even then, the result is usually friendship and rarely conversion or church planting. Humanitarian aid/social action must be combined with other avenues to reach a particular people group, like witnessing to members of that people who live in open countries.[65]

McGavran's Understanding of the Goal for Missions and Understanding of Suffering in Missions

McGavran's understanding of the goal of missions is similar to Piper in the sense that both desire to win people from all people groups to Christ. However, they differ in emphasis because McGavran focuses on the multiplication of churches in receptive areas and Piper centers on the glory of God. McGavran believes the task of evangelism will only be complete when in "every part of every country a church is established in every community."[66] McGavran states that if a missionary's focus is not on the multiplication of churches in "all the nations," work will center on humanitarianism

---

63 Donald McGavran, "Contemporary Evangelical Theology of Mission," in Arthur F. Glasser and Donald McGavran, eds., *Contemporary Theologies of Mission* (Grand Rapids: Baker, 1983), 103.

64 McGavran, *Understanding Church Growth*, 26, 89, 292; McGavran, *Bridges of God*, 53–59.

65 Donald McGavran, "Barred Populations and Missionaries," *International Review of Mission* 64 (Jan 1975): 60.

66 McGavran, *How Churches Grow*, 38.

or academics, not evangelism.[67] McGavran believes several Scriptures used together show God's desire for the church to win peoples to grow churches exponentially. John 17:18 states the reason for sending Christians into the world is that the lost may believe. Acts 1:8 emphasizes evangelism of the world. Galatians 1:6 states that God told Paul to proclaim Christ to the Gentiles. In Rom 1:5–6, Paul explains that his call centered on bringing faith and obedience to people of all people groups. Romans 16:25–27 states that the gospel is supposed to bring all the people groups to God.[68] Matthew 28:16–20, the Church Growth School's "favorite text,"[69] states that discipleship and church membership are the "chief and irreplaceable duty and privilege of all Christians."[70]

The culmination of McGavran's missiology rests in the multiplication of churches in receptive homogeneous peoples. Christians need to focus where God is working. He believes each people have an opportune time for salvation.[71] Christians must focus on responsive peoples, as the disciples began with common Jews, expanded to Levites, and then to God-fearing Gentiles.[72] In uninterested or unresponsive peoples, missionaries must "shake the dust of their feet" (Matt 10:14; Acts 13:46–51) and move to a receptive people,[73] and leave only a remnant behind. Those who remain must make proper preparations for when that people becomes responsive.[74]

McGavran cites several factors that may change receptivity and aid church growth. People in new settlements are usually free

---

67 McGavran, *Understanding Church Growth*, 22, 413.
68 McGavran, *Ten Steps for Church Growth*, 35–39.
69 David Smith, "The Church Growth Principles of Donald McGavran," *Transformation* 2, no. 2 (April/June 1985): 26.
70 McGavran, *Ten Steps for Church Growth*, 37.
71 McGavran, *Understanding Church Growth*, 124.
72 McGavran, *Ten Steps for Church Growth*, 39; and McGavran, *Church Growth and Christian Mission*, 74.
73 McGavran, *Church Growth and Christian Mission*, 82; and McGavran, *Momentous Decisions*, 57.
74 McGavran, *Understanding Church Growth*, 262.

from old traditions and are open to new thoughts; they also desire friendships and community. Those who return from traveling abroad may have gained new insight on their old environment. Conquered peoples may be more open to their liberator's faith. If the church affirms government during a time of increasing nationalism, it may gain a hearing. When people are free from controls that hinder the spread of the gospel, they are more apt to listen and respond. When societies interact and adapt to new situations (acculturation), people are more receptive.[75]

McGavran does not discuss suffering as it relates to missions. He focuses on church growth and witnessing to receptive people groups. Suffering in missions is not a priority. McGavran is practical and pragmatic in his thoughts and actions, and his strategies focused on the situations of his day.

---

75   Ibid., 248–56.

8

THE WILL OF GOD

INTRODUCTION

The last couple of chapters centered on Piper's understanding of missions. They explained the key components and compared Piper with a couple respected missiologists. This chapter and the next focus on the idea of the "will of God." I will begin with defining what the will of God is and the Two Wills of God Thesis. Then I will address the problem of evil in relation of God. The next chapter will tackle Piper's understanding of God's will in relation the to Two Wills of God Thesis, which will show how Piper reconciles his Calvinism with missions.

THE WILL OF GOD DEFINED

Theologians generally agree that defining God's will centers on his sovereignty or being. According to Louis Berkof, the will of God is the "perfection of His Being whereby He, in a most simple act, goes out toward Himself as the highest good (i.e. delights in Himself as such) and towards His creatures for His own name's sake, and this is the ground of their being and continued existence."[1] Thomas Oden defines the will of God as, "[T]he infinite power of God to determine God's own intentions, execute actions, and use means adequate to the ends intended."[2] Charles Hodge sees God's will as his self-determination, power, and moral attri-

---

1   Louis Berkof, *Systematic Theology*, 4th rev. and expanded ed. (Grand Rapids: Eerdmans, 1941; reprint, 1996), 76–77, italics his.
2   Thomas C. Oden, *The Living God: Systematic Theology: Volume One* (Peabody, MA: Prince, 2001), 90.

butes.[3] James Arminius names the actions of divine providence or will as, "Wisdom, Goodness, Justice, Severity and Power."[4]

Similarly, regarding the definition of the wills of God, the Two Wills of God Thesis is a popular explanation,[5] though many would not label their understanding as such or use that terminology. John Gill states there is one will of God, but it is distinguished into several elements that may appear contradictory though they are in harmony.[6] Calvin agrees the wills of God are in symmetry even amid apparent conflict.[7] Jonathan Edwards states that the wills of God are not contradictory because while each component may have the same subject, each part has a different focus.[8] Arminius distinguished between God's will of "good pleasure" and will of "open intimation."[9] Charles Finney realizes there is a distinction between God's "secret purpose" and revealed will.[10] Systematic theologian Dale Moody believes there is a difference

---

3   Charles Hodge, *Systematic Theology*, vol. 1 (Grand Rapids: Eerdmans; reprint, Peabody, MA: Hendrickson, 2003), 402.

4   James Arminius, *The Works of Arminius*, vol. 2, trans. James Nichols and William Nichols (reprint, Grand Rapids: Baker, 1986), 368.

5   For example: Clark Pinnock, *Grace Unlimited* (Minneapolis: Bethany Fellowship, 1975), 13; Randall G. Basinger, "Exhaustive Divine Sovereignty," in *A Case for Arminianism*, ed. Clark Pinnock (Grand Rapids: Zondervan, 1898), 96; and R. T. Forster and V. P. Marston, *God's Strategy in Human Strategy* (Wheaton: Tyndale, 1973), 32.

6   John Gill, *A Complete Body of Doctrinal and Practical Divinity* (reprint, Paris, AR: Baptist Standard Bearer, 1999), cd rom, 174.

7   John Calvin, *Secret Providence*, trans. James Lillie (1840; reprint, Albany, OR: Ages Software, 1998), cd rom, 44, 48.

8   Jonathan Edwards, "Concerning the Decrees in General, and Election in Particular," in *The Works of Jonathan Edwards*, vol. 2 (New York: Leavitt &Allen, 1855; reprint, Edinburgh: Banner of Truth Trust, 1974), 546. See also: Calvin, *Secret Providence*, 44, 48; Hodge, *Systematic Theology*, 402–04; Berkof, Systematic Theology, 79; Wayne Grudem, *Systematic Theology* (Grand Rapids: Zondervan, 1994), 343.

9   Arminius, *The Works of Arminius*, 344–45.

10   Charles Finney, *Finney's Systematic Theology*, comp. and ed. Dennis Carroll, Bill Nicely, L. G. Parkhurst, new expanded ed. (Minneapolis: Bethany, 1994), 496.

between God's purpose or "good pleasure," which is certain and determined, and God's permissive will, which may be uncertain and indefinite.[11]

Definition and Explanation of the Two Wills of God Thesis

The Two Wills of God Thesis simply notes the idea that God has more than one way of willing. There are various terms that categorize the distinctions in God's will. Two phrases often associated with this differentiation are "secret will" and "revealed will." The secret will is also referred to the will of decree, sovereign will, decretive will, purposing will, *voluntas signi* (will of sign), and hidden will.[12] The revealed will is associated with the will of command, moral will, preceptive will, *voluntas bebeplaciti* (will of good pleasure), and commanding will.[13]

The secret will is God's unchangeable purpose. It is known only by God and cannot be frustrated. The hidden will regulates things unknown in Scripture. People cannot violate God's hidden will; they will obey it.[14] Arminius explains the will of God's good pleasure is "irresistible;" God will "strictly and rigidly" secure it.[15] Hodge believes God's secret will determines what God will do and what he will permit.[16] Gill states one's death, salvation, judgment, and the second coming of Christ all fall under the secret will of God.[17] Calvin maintains that God rules creation by his secret will. He cites Rom 11:33–34 and Isa 40:13–14 that state no one can understand God and call the way God rules the world a mystery.[18] Elsewhere, Calvin states God rules a person's actions by his secret

---

11 Dale Moody, *The Word of Truth: A Summary of Christian Doctrine Based on Biblical Revelation* (Grand Rapids: Eerdmans, 1981), 152–53.

12 Berkof, *Systematic Theology*, 77–79

13 Ibid.

14 Millard Erickson, *Christian Theology*, 2d ed. (Grand Rapids: Baker, 1998), 303.

15 Arminius, *The Works of Arminius*, 345.

16 Hodge, *Systematic Theology*, 403–04.

17 Gill, *A Complete Body of Doctrinal and Practical Divinity*, 176–77.

18 Calvin, *Institutes*, 212–13.

will and permits them to make mistakes and deviate from truth.[19] Finney understands creation comes under God's secret will.[20] Deuteronomy 29:29, Ps 115:3, and Rom 9:18-19 are some Scripture passages that reflect the sovereign will of God.[21]

God's revealed will conveys guidelines in Scripture.[22] Finney believes God's revealed will can be transgressed even though God is in control of events.[23] Erickson and Berkof explain God's preceptive will is like God's wish; God desires something to happen, but does not necessarily ordain or decree it.[24] Gill maintains the commanding will of God shows God's desires and, therefore, leaves people without excuse to follow God.[25] Oden cites Thomas Aquinas' five marks through which God makes known the revealed will:

» operations—when God works to effect something
» permissions—when God allows something
» precepts—when God positively commands an action
» prohibitions—when God negates or negatively requires something not to be enacted
» counsels—when God teaches or advises but does not coerce an action.[26]

Deuteronomy 30:14, Matt 7:21, and Rom 10:8 are some Scripture passages that represent the revealed will of God.[27]

Erasmus and Luther also acknowledge God has separate ways of willing. Luther specifically distinguishes between God's secret

---

19   Calvin, *Secret Providence*, 34, 46, 56.
20   Finney, *Finney's Systematic Theology*, 486–87.
21   Osterhaven, "Will of God," 1277.
22   Ibid.
23   Finney, *Finney's Systematic Theology*, 491–96.
24   Erickson, *Christian Doctrine*, 387; Berkof, *Systematic Theology*, 77–78.
25   Gill, *A Complete Body of Doctrinal and Practical Divinity*, 176–77.
26   Thomas Aquinas, *Summa Theologica*, vol. 1, ed. English Dominican Fathers (New York: Benziger, 1947), 103; quoted in Oden, *The Living God*, 95–96.
27   Osterhaven, "Will of God," 1277.

and revealed wills. He states that God reveals his will in Scripture.[28] This will may not be obeyed, as in the case of the general call to salvation. God's hidden will is what he "ordains" to occur. This will is kept secret from humans and not revealed in Scripture. Luther criticizes Erasmus for not using the terms "secret will" and "revealed will;"[29] however, Erasmus does believe God wills differently. According to Erasmus, God frequently uses a person's actions to further God's will in a separate way than he intended.[30]

The two wills of God are not isolated from one another. They cooperate with each other, especially when dealing with humankind. Since God's will is always good and a person's desires are often evil, the two sometimes conflict. When God's revealed will and a person's desires do not agree, the person sins against God, but God's secret will is still accomplished. Finney cites Joseph, the Assyrian king, and Jesus as examples. Joseph, sold into slavery by his brothers (a violation of God's revealed will), preserved Jacob's clan—the future Israel—from starvation (God's secret will). God used the Assyrian king, who desired to destroy Israel completely (a violation of God's revealed will) to punish Israel for the purpose of restoration (God's secret will). Pilate gave the orders to crucify Christ (a violation of God's revealed will) in order that God may provide salvation to those who love him (God's secret will).[31] Gill concurs with Finney.[32]

EXCURSUS 1: THE SECRET WILL AND THE PROBLEM OF EVIL

A related issue to the Two Wills of God Thesis is the problem of sin and evil. Theologians agree that God permits evil; however, they disagree about the role that God plays in evil. Augustine states that sin enters the world to promote something superior—

---

28   Luther, "On the Bondage of the Will," 200–01.

29   Ibid., 201

30   Erasmus, "On the Freedom of the Will," 67.

31   Finney, *Finney's Systematic Theology*, 487–88, 492–93.

32   Gill, *A Complete Body of Doctrinal and Practical Divinity*, 176–77.

God's glory. Stephen Charnock espouses a common belief that God wills sin/evil to exist through secondary or immediate causes. In other words, God does not positively ordain sin/evil, but he wills other events that cause sin. However, some theologians do not accept this idea. Bruce Reichenbach believes that because God created people with a free will, God cannot prevent people from choosing sin/evil. Pinnock explains that God can only condemn people's sin if people are completely free.[33]

When the problem of sin/evil is discussed, there are normally three types of sin/evil mentioned:[34] metaphysical,[35] moral,[36] and

---

33 For more information see: Augustine, *Enchiridion* IV–IX, *The Library of Christian Classics*, vol. 7, eds. John Baillie, John T. McNeill, and Henry P. van Dusen (Philadelphia: Westminster: 1959), 342–59; Steven Charnock, *The Existence and Attributes of God*, vol 1, (Grand Rapids: Baker, 2000), 148; orig. pub. as *Discourses Upon the Existence of and Attributes of God* (Robert Carter and Brothers: New York, 1853), 533; Charnock, *The Existence and Attributes of God*, vol. 2, 148–49; Jonathan Edwards, *Freedom of the Will*, in *The Works of President Edwards*, vol. 2, 9th ed (New York: Leavitt & Allen, 1855; reprint), 160; John Feinberg, *No One Like Him: The Doctrine of God* (Wheaton: Crossway, 2001), 696; Berkof, *Systematic Theology*, 220; Gill, A Complete Body of Doctrinal and Practical Divinity, 181; Bruce R. Reinchenbach, *Evil and a Good God* (New York: Fordham University Press, 1982), 64; Reichenbach, "God Limits His Power," 111–12; and Pinnock, "God Limits His Knowledge," 156–58.

34 Norman Geisler, "Evil, Problem Of," in *Baker Encyclopedia of Christian Apologetics* (Grand Rapids: Baker, 1999), 219. See also John S. Feinberg, *No One Like Him: The Doctrine of God* (Wheaton: Crossway, 2001), 778, who uses the terms "religious problem of evil," "philosophical problem of evil" or "moral evil," and "natural evil," respectively.

35 Norman Geisler and Winfried Corduan, Philosophy of Religion, 2d ed. (Grand Rapids: Baker, 1988), 314, state the question of metaphysical evil is:
   1. God is the author of everything in the world
   2. Evil is something in the world.
   3. Therefore, God is the author of evil.

36 Ibid. Moral evil is:
   1. Evil exists.
   2. An omniscient God could destroy evil.
   3. A benevolent God would destroy evil.

physical.[37] Questions usually surround metaphysical and moral evil, not physical evil.[38] Theologians agree on the reasons for God's ordination/permission of evil. Gill and Calvin explain that God wills to use evil against humankind in two ways: chastisement/ punishment and sin. God chastises his children and punishes unbelievers. Chastisement is part of God's will because it is congruous with God's attributes of "justice, holiness, wisdom, love, and goodness."[39] Chastisement is part of the sanctification process. Gill explains that punishment of the unregenerate is part of God's will because it glorifies the justice of God.[40] Calvin agrees and states: "God accomplished his own design: wisely employing like one supremely good, even evil, for the damnation of those, whom he justly predestinated to punishment."[41]

Oden states that pain is used to grow the Christian: "Chastisement and discipline are offices of the Holy Spirit (gifts of God), seeking to cleanse and make chaste our spirits and educate our moral sense."[42] Geisler implicitly agrees when he states God uses suffering "to get our attention."[43] According to E. Y. Mull-

---

 4. Therefore, since evil is not destroyed, then either
  a. God is omniscient and hence malevolent in some way, or
  b. God is benevolent and hence impotent in some way, or
  c. God is both malevolent and impotent, or
  d. there is not God at all
37 Ibid. Geisler and Corduan use the idea of a plague in Albert Camus's novel to capture the question of physical evil:
  1. Either one must join the doctor and fight the plague or else join the priest and not fight the plague.
  2. Not to fight the plague is anti-humanitarian.
  3. To fight the plague is to fight against God who sent it.
  4. Therefore, if humanitarianism is right, theism is wrong.
38 Feinberg, *No One Like Him*, 778.
39 Gill, *A Complete Body of Doctrinal and Practical Divinity*, 179. See also Calvin, *Secret Providence*, 33.
40 Gill, *A Complete Body of Doctrinal and Practical Divinity*, 179.
41 Calvin, *Secret Providence*, 31.
42 Thomas Oden, *The Word of Life: Systematic Theology: Volume Two* (San Francisco, 1989), 425.
43 Geisler, "Evil, Problem Of," 223.

ins, the final punishment for unbelievers is eternal hell and it is the "only rational outcome of unbelief and sin."[44] Arminius states that "God wills the evils of punishment, because he would rather have the order of Justice preserved in punishment, than to suffer an offending creature to go unpunished."[45]

Sin/evil occurs when the revealed will of God is violated. Stephen Charnock asserts a common belief by many Calvinists that God wills sin/evil to exist through secondary or immediate causes. God does not positively ordain sin/evil; God wills other events that cause sin.[46] Gill agrees and states: "God may be said, is such senses, to will sin, yet he wills it in a different way than he wills that which is good; he does not will to do it himself, nor to do it by others; but permits it to be done; and which is not a bare permission, but a voluntary permission; and is expressed by God 'giving' up men to their own hearts' lusts."[47]

There is a reason for God permitting sin.[48] Edwards provides a fluid explanation:

> It is a proper and excellent thing for infinite glory to shine forth; and for the same reason, it is proper that the shining forth of God's glory should be complete; that is, that all parts of his glory should shine forth, that every beauty should be proportionally effulgent, that the beholder may have a proper notion of God. It is not proper that one glory should be exceedingly manifested, and another not at all.
>
> Thus it is necessary, that God's awful majesty, his authority and dreadful greatness, justice, and holiness, should be manifested. But this could not be, unless sin and pun-

---

44 E. Y. Mullins, *The Christian Religion in Its Doctrinal Expression* (Nashville: Sunday School Board of the Southern Baptist Convention, 1917), 489.

45 Arminius, *The Works of Arminius*, 130.

46 Charnock, *The Existence and Attributes of God*, 149.

47 Gill, *A Complete Body of Doctrinal and Practical Divinity*, 181.

48 Augustine, *Enchiridion IV–IX*, in John Baillie, John T. McNeill, and Henry P. van Dusen, eds., *The Library of Christian Classics*, vol. 7 (Philadelphia: Westminster: 1954), 342–59.

ishment had been decreed; so that the shining forth of
God's glory would be very imperfect, both because these
parts of divine glory would not shine forth as the others
do, and also the glory of his goodness, love, and holiness
would be faint without them; nay, they could scarcely
shine forth at all.

So evil is necessary, in order to the highest happiness of
the creature, and the completeness of that communica-
tion of God, for which he made the world; because the
creature's happiness consists in the knowledge of God,
and the sense of his love. And if the knowledge of him
be imperfect, the happiness of the creature must be proportionally imperfect.[49]

Norman Geisler and Winfried Corduan accept this idea of
God's sovereignty because it can allow for free will. state:

But such a Calvinist does not (nor need he) deny that human beings have a will, the capability of making choices, or moral responsibility. These are notions that are
often put into the mouths by their opponents, but not
even hyper-Calvinists would say that humans are mere
puppets. For them, the ultimate theological authority is
Scripture, which affirms a human will, human choices,
and human responsibility. What they are not willing to
do is draw the rational inference from there to a free will,
free choices, and responsibility based on significant freedom."[50]

---

49 Jonathan Edwards; quoted in Piper, "Is God Less Glorious Because He
    Ordained that Evil Be?"
50 Geisler and Corduan, *Philosophy of Religion*, 337–38.

9

PIPER AND THE TWO WILLS OF GOD THESIS

INTRODUCTION

Piper believes God has a revealed will and a secret will. The revealed will is found only in Scripture and can be disobeyed and broken;[1] the secret will is God's complete governance over all events.[2] In relation to Piper's understanding of the glory of God in missions, he uses the Two Wills of God Thesis to distinguish between what God "would like to see happen" (revealed will) and what God "wills to happen" (secret will): both are part of God's glory. Some of the tenants of Christian Hedonism are seen in both wills in relation to missions. In the revealed will, missions is seen in God's desire to save the world—God's desire for every person to be saved. In the secret will, missions is seen in God's power to save the elect and give the missionary hope in the midst of suffering.

Piper believes the revealed will of God can be known, accomplished, and broken.[3] When a person reacts to a situation, consciously or unconsciously, the revealed will of God is either obeyed or broken. Piper cites 1 Thess 4:3; 5:18, and 1 John 2:17 as examples of the revealed will. First Thessalonians 4:3 states part of God's will for the Christian life is sanctification, but he sins daily.

---

1   John Piper, "What Is the Will of God and How Do We Know It?," <http://www.desiringgod.org/library/sermons/04/082204.html>, site editor, Desiring God Ministries, August 22, 2004, accessed on 18 October 2004.

2   Ibid.

3   This is different than divination, which requires new revelation rather than a renewed mind, something Piper does not believe necessary in seeking God's will.

First Thessalonians 5:18 explains that the Christian is always to give thanks, but he does not. First John 2:17 states that God's will is for everyone to "abide forever," but only those in Christ have eternal life.[4]

Piper states people do not know (and are not supposed to know or seek) the secret will of God. This will is God's alone to know. Deuteronomy 29:29 states that the secret things belong to God.[5] Matthew 26:39, a reference to Christ's desire to be saved from the cross, states "not as I will, but as you will." The second will mentioned is God's will of decree; it will happen.[6] Ephesians 1:11 states God's will controls all things, even ordinary events. The secret will of God is easily seen in the problem of evil and the doctrine of election.

Piper believes the revealed and secret wills of God are not isolated from one another, even when they seem incompatible. This is seen especially with evil and missions. He uses some of the same examples already mentioned. Joseph, sold into slavery by his brothers (a violation of God's revealed will), saved the lives of many people (God's secret will). At the crucifixion, Herod, Pilate, the soldiers, and Jewish leaders accomplished God's secret will in sinning (a violation of God's revealed will) by sending Christ to die on the cross.[7] Eli's sons violated the revealed will of God by disobeying their parents; God desired to kill them (secret will) for their rebelliousness.[8]

The idea of the two wills does not fall into a single theological camp. He states, "The distinction between terms like 'will of decree' and 'will of command' or 'sovereign will' and 'moral will'

---

4   Piper, "What Is the Will of God and How Do We Know It?"
5   Piper, "Pastoral Thoughts on the Doctrine of Election;" and Piper, "Fulfilling the Law of Love: Education for Exaltation: Through the Spirit by Faith," <http://www. desiringgod.org/library/sermons/00/022700. html>, site editor, Desiring God Ministries, February 27, 2000, accessed on 3 February 2004.
6   Piper, "What is the Will of God and How Do We Know It?"
7   Piper, "Is God Less Glorious Because He Ordained that Evil Be?"
8   Piper, *The Pleasures of God*, 324–25.

is not an artificial division demanded by Calvinistic theology. The terms are an effort to describe the whole of biblical revelation."[9] The difference between Arminians and Calvinists lie in their understanding of salvation. Both realize God desires to save all and does not. Arminians believe the reason is because God gives a person the ability to or not to choose God. Calvinists state the reason is because God seeks his own glory.[10]

THE REVEALED WILL, GOD'S UNIVERSAL LOVE, AND MISSIONS

The universal love of God is given to all and demonstrates how God gives all people life and treats all people fairly.[11] This is called common grace. Common grace is God's grace given to all and shows God's love for the world.[12] This is seen clearest in God making every person in his own image, both the elect and the unregenerate. Since each individual is made in the image of God, each individual is in some sense like God.[13] Though God's image in humanity is warped by sin, people have the ability in some sense to glorify God.[14] Only when a person dies without Christ is there no chance to magnify God's greatness;[15] and even then the person glorifies God's justice in hell.[16] God's image shines[17] in a

9   Ibid., 331–33.

10   Ibid., 333.

11   Piper, "Those Whom He Predestined He Also Called: Part One."

12   Philip E. Hughes, "Grace," in *Evangelical Dictionary of Theology*, 2d ed. , ed Walter A. Elwell (Grand Rapids: Baker, 2001), 519–22.

13   John Piper, "He is Like a Refiner's Fire," <http://www.desiringgod.org/ library/sermons/87/112987.html>, site editor, Desiring God Ministries, November 29, 1987, accessed on 9 November 2004.

14   John Piper, "He is Like a Refiner's Fire," <http://www.desiringgod.org/ library/sermons/87/112987.html>, site editor, Desiring God Ministries, November 29, 1987, accessed on 9 November 2004.

15   John Piper, "Heart's Desire," <http://www.desiringgod.org/library/sermons/85/010685.html>, site editor, Desiring God Ministries, January 6, 1985, accessed on 24 February 2003.

16   Piper, "Behold the Kindness and Severity of God."

17   Piper, "Male and Female He Created Them in the Image of God."

world of sin because he desires that "people in his image fill the earth with his glory."[18] Piper stresses this point when he states:

> No matter what the skin color or facial features or hair texture or other genetic traits, every human being in every ethnic group has an immortal soul in the image of God: a mind with unique, God–like reasoning powers, a heart with capacities for moral judgments and spiritual affections, and a potential for relationship with God that sets every person utterly apart from all the animals which God has made. Every human being, whatever color, shape, age, gender, intelligence, health or social class, is made in the image of God.[19]

This is one reason God has compassion on cities like Nineveh and calls Jonah to proclaim his message and give them an opportunity to repent and submit to God.[20]

Common grace is also seen in government and human conscience. God could have let the world run on its own, but he is directly involved in its affairs.[21] He allows unbelievers sometimes to act like believers. God in some sense takes pleasure in the godly characteristics the unregenerate display. However, since these

---

18   John Piper, "God's Covenant with Noah," <http://www.desiringgod.org/library/sermons/83/112786.html>, site editor, Desiring God Ministries, November 27, 1983, accessed on 9 November 2004.

19   John Piper, "The Mission and Vision of Bethlehem Baptist Church Volume Twelve: Racial Reconciliation Unpacking the Master Planning Team Document Unfolding Fresh Initiative Three Fresh Initiatives for the Immediate Future of Our Mission," <http://www.desiringgod.org/library/sermons/96/011496.html>, site editor, Desiring God Ministries, January 11, 1996, accessed on 9 November 2004.

20   John Piper, "The Day of Praise Procession Part Two: Should Not I Pity That Great City—Minneapolis?," <http://www.desiringgod.org/library/sermons/92/ 060792.html>, site editor, Desiring God Ministries, June 6, 1992, accessed on 9 November 2004.

21   Piper, The Pleasures of God, 256. See also: John Piper, "Jesus Christ: Alive and with Us to the End," <http://www.desiringgod.org/library/sermons/00/041200.html>, site editor, Desiring God Ministries, April 12, 2000, accessed on 1 November 2004.

characteristics are done apart from faith, they are sin.[22] Piper uses the analogy of a seashell washed upon the shore and states while there is no life is the seashell (unbeliever), it does have a type of attractiveness (non-believer's "good" actions).[23]

The universal love of God relates to God's revealed will by way of Christian Hedonism. This is seen clearly in the basic premise: "God is most glorified in us when we are most satisfied in him."[24] All people, including the unregenerate, desire satisfaction, though unregenerate people search for satisfaction in things that are fleeting.[25] He quotes Pascal: "Whatever different means they employ, they all tend to this end [satisfaction]. . . . The will never takes the least step but to this object. This is the motive of every action of every man, even of those who hang themselves."[26]

Piper cites Scriptures stressing God's commandments to find joy in him because rejoicing in God is obeying God.[27] Psalm 37:4, Ps 100:2, and other passages[28] command delighting in

---

22 John Piper, "The Pleasure of God in Public Justice,"<http://www.desir-inggod.org/library/sermons/87/040587.html>, site editor, Desiring God Ministries, April 5, 1987, accessed on 1 November 2004.

23 Piper, *The Pleasures of God*, 256.

24 "Who is Desiring God," <http://www.desiringgod.org/who_is_dgm_index. html>, site editor, Desiring God Ministries, accessed on 24 November 2004. The Desiring God website, www.desiringgod.org, has this phrase listed over 2300 times.

25 John Piper, "A Response to Richard Mouw's Treatment of Christian Hedonism in *The God Who Commands*," <http://www.desiringgod.org/library/topics/christian_ hedonism/mouw.html>, site editor, Desiring God Ministries, accessed on 08 January 2004, is not saying that actions are worshipful or even correct because they evoke pleasure. Nor is he saying that pleasure involves love. Instead, he states the distinctive characteristic of Christian Hedonism is "love [and worship] requires [sic] true happiness."

26 Blaise Pascal; quoted in Piper, "A Response to Richard Mouw's Treatment of Christian Hedonism in *The God Who Commands*."

27 Piper, "Treating Delight as Duty is Controversial."

28 There are plenty of other passages that state God commands people to be happy such as: Ps 32:11; 37:4; 66:1–2; 67:4; 97:12; Matt 22:37; and Luke 10:20. See: "What Do You Think About the Notion that

God.[29] Deuteronomy 28:47–48 states terrible things will occur if a person is not happy in God.[30] Piper uses some of these passages in his evangelistic tract, "Quest for Joy." He believes that the command found in Ps 37:4, "Delight yourself in the Lord and he will give you the desires of your heart," is the first thing a person must do.[31] The nature of salvation involves "loving God (Matthew 22:37) and trusting him (1 John 5:3–4) and being thankful to him (Psalm 100:2–4)."[32]

Piper also notes that everyone has responsibility to find joy in Christ even those who are not elect. Romans leaves everyone without excuse. Romans 1–2 explain that natural revelation tells people about God.[33] Romans 3 and 6 state that everyone has fall-

---

God is Concerned About Our Holiness Rather than Our Happiness," <http://www.desiringgod.org/library/theological_qa/chr_hedonism/holiness _happiness.html>, site editor, Desiring God Ministries, accessed on 29 November 2004; and John Piper, "Treating Delight as Duty is Controversial," <http://www.desiringgod. org/library/fresh_words/2001/102401.html>, site editor, Desiring God Ministries, October 24, 2001, accessed on 29 November 2004.

29   John Piper, "Loving God for Who He Is: A Pastor's Perspective," <http://www.desiringgod.org/topics/leadership/loving_god.html>, site editor, Desiring God Ministries, accessed on 29 November 2004; John Piper, "Joy Through the Fiery Test of Faith," <http://www.desiringgod.org/library/sermons/93/102493.html>, site editor, Desiring God Ministries, October 24, 1993, accessed on 29 November 2004; and John Piper, "Take Care How You Listen!," <http://www.desiringgod.org/ library/sermons/98/022298.html>, site editor, Desiring God Ministries, February 22, 1998, accessed on 29 November 2004.

30   Piper, *Desiring God*, 294, 368.

31   Piper, *Quest for Joy*. See also: Piper, Desiring God, 55; and John Piper, "Quest: Joy. Found: Christ," <http://www.desiringgod.org/library/sermons/03/042003.html>, site editor, Desiring God Ministries, April 20, 2003, accessed on 29 November 2004.

32   John Piper, "Quest for Joy: Six Biblical Truths," <http://www.desiringgod.org/library/what_we_believe/quest4joy.html>, site editor, Desiring God Ministries, accessed on 21 November 2004.

33   John Piper, "There is No Partiality with God [Part One]," <http://www.desiringgod.org/library/sermons/98/122798.html>, site editor, Desiring God Ministries, December 27, 1998, accessed on 29 November 2004

en into sin and hope is found only in Jesus.[34] Romans 10:14–15 states that God sends messengers to proclaim the gospel to those who have not believed in order that they may come to Christ.[35]

In other passages such as John 14:6, Piper comments that Jesus is the only way to heaven.[36] In discussing John 3:16, Piper

and John Piper, "There is No Partiality with God: Part Two," <http://www.desiringgod.org/library/sermons/90/ 011399.html>, site editor, Desiring God Ministries, January 13, 1999, accessed on 29 November 2004.

34 Piper addresses this subject extensively For example: John Piper, "The Demonstration of God's Righteousness: Justification and Mother's Day," <http://www.desiringgod.org/library/sermons/99/050999.html>, site editor, Desiring God Ministries, May 5, 1999, accessed on 29 November 2004; John Piper, "The Demonstration of God's Righteousness: Part Two," <http://www.desiring god.org/library/sermons/99/051699.html>, site editor, Desiring God Ministries, May 16, 1999, accessed on 29 November 2004; John Piper, "The Demonstration of God's Righteousness: Part Three," <http://www.desiringgod.org/library/sermons/99/ 052399. html>, site editor, Desiring God Ministries, May 23, 1999, accessed on 29 November 2004; John Piper, "The Free Gift of God is Eternal Life: Part One," <http://www.desiringgod.org/library/ sermons/00/121700. html>, site editor, Desiring God Ministries, December 17, 2000, accessed on 29 November 2004; and John Piper, "The Free Gift of God is Eternal Life: Part Two," <http://www.desiringgod.org/ library/sermons/00/122400.html>, site editor, Desiring God Ministries, December 24, 2000, accessed on 29 November 2004.

35 Piper, "How Shall People Be Saved: Part 2."

36 Again, Piper addresses this subject as well. For example: John Piper, "Not Ashamed of the Gospel," <http://www.desiringgod.org/library/sermons/ 98/060498.html>, site editor, Desiring God Ministries, June 4, 1998, accessed on 29 November 2004; John Piper, "An Open Letter to Rabbi Marcia Zimmerman," <http://www.desiringgod.org/ library/freshwords/2004/030304.html>, site editor, Desiring God Ministries, March 3, 2004, accessed on 29 November 2004; John Piper, "What Happens When You Die: At Home with the Lord," <http://www.desiring god.org/ library/sermons/93/ 071893.html>, site editor, Desiring God Ministries, July 18, 1993, accessed on 29 November 2004; John Piper, "What the Law Could Not Do, God Did, Sending Christ," <http://www. desiringgod.org/library/sermons/01/101401.html>, site editor, Desiring God Ministries, October 10, 2001, accessed on 29 November 2004; John Piper, "I Will Build My Church—From All Peoples," <http://www.

states that belief is essential; saving faith is "the vital link between your soul and God's rescuing love."[37] Galatians 6:10 states that one reason why one shows kindness toward non-believers is in order that they will come to Christ.[38]

Piper not only maintains that every person is responsible to find joy in Christ, he believes that God desires every person to find joy in Christ: finding joy in Christ is salvation.[39] Ezekiel 18:23; 32 state that God does not enjoy seeing the death of the wicked.[40] The death and suffering and destruction of humans, even unregenerate ones, in a temporal sense, dishonors God.[41] Luke 13:34 (also Matt 23:37) states Christ cried over the unbelief of Jerusalem. God grieves over her because sin dishonors God and demonstrates hatred toward him. Luke 19:41–44 (and other pas-

---

desiringgod.org/library/sermons/01/102801.html>, site editor, Desiring God Ministries, October 28, 2001, accessed on 29 November 2004; and Piper, "There is Salvation in No One Else."

37   John Piper, "The Duty: Faith," <http://desiringgod.org/library/sermons/94/ 121894.html>, site editor, Desiring God Ministries, December 18, 1994, accessed 13 March 2003.

38   John Piper, "Doing Mercy to the Brothers of Jesus and the Broken Neighbor," <http://www.desiringgod.org/library/sermons/04/100304.html>, site editor, Desiring God Ministries, October 4, 2004, accessed on 21 November 2004.

39   Piper, *Desiring God*, 352–53.

40   Piper, "Those Whom He Predestined He Also Called: Part 2;" and Piper, "Heart's Desire."

41   John Piper, "Is There Good Anxiety," <http://www.desiringgod.org/library/sermons/81/042181.html>, site editor, Desiring God Ministries, April 21, 1981, accessed on 14 December 2004. Piper is clear that eternally God is not dishonored by sin because God sees sin bringing glory to his justice. He explains: "God's grief over sin and condemnation is owing, therefore, to His ability to view sin and condemnation as ends in themselves, which thus considered are grievous. But He is not an eternally unhappy or frustrated God because He can and does view sin and condemnation in relation to the universality of things where it is considered not for its ends but for God's ultimate ends through its existence. When God looks at the totality of redemptive history in this way, He rejoices at what He sees, with even sin and condemnation resounding to His great glory."

sages such as Phil 3:18; Rom 9:1–3; 10:1) state all the people of Jerusalem had to do was accept the terms of peace Jesus offered.[42] Luke 19:41–42 shows as Christ cried over the "lostness" of Jerusalem, Christians should feel remorse for those failing to receive Christ.[43] Piper even gives credence to the interpretations of 1 Tim 2:11 and 2 Pet 3:9 that state God desires to see all people come to Christ[44] and that in some sense Christ died for every person.[45]

Piper stresses that anyone who desires may have eternal life. He makes clear this means anyone. Revelation 22 "throw[s] out the Great Invitation as widely as it possibly can to all men and women and children everywhere,"[46] he writes. Romans 10:13 states that whomever calls upon God's name will become a Chris-

---

42   John Piper, "O, That You Knew the Terms of Peace," <http://www.desiringgod.org/library/sermons/81/041281.html>, site editor, Desiring God Ministries, April 12, 1981, accessed on 20 November 2004.

43   John Piper, "Tolerance, Truth-telling, Violence, and Law: Principles for How Christians Should Relate to Those of Other Faiths: Spreading a Passion for the Supremacy of Jesus Christ in a Pluralistic and Hostile World Where National Identity and Religious Identity Are Blurred," <http://www.desiringgod.org/library/topics/culture/tolerance_principles.html>, site editor, Desiring God Ministries, accessed on 20 November 2004. See also: John Piper, "Can Christians Be Held Hostage By the Sins of the Beloved?," <<http://www.desiringgod.org/library/fresh_words/ 1999/030999.html>, site editor, Desiring God Ministries, March 9, 1999, accessed on 20 November 2004.

44   John Piper, "There is No Partiality with God [Part One]," <http://www.desiringgod.org/library/sermons/98/122798.html>, site editor, Desiring God Ministries, December 27, 1998, accessed on 29 November 2004 and John Piper, "There is No Partiality with God: Part Two," <http://www.desiringgod.org/library/sermons/90/ 011399.html>, site editor, Desiring God Ministries, January 13, 1999, accessed on 29 November 2004.

45   Piper, "For Whom Did Jesus Taste Death?;" Piper, "Those Whom He Predestined He Also Called: Part Two;" and Piper, "What We Believe About the Five Points of Calvinism."

46   John Piper, "The Great Invitation: Break Forth in Song!," <http://www.desiringgod.org/library/sermons/88/082888.html>, site editor, Desiring God Ministries, August 28, 1988, accessed on 21 November 2004.

tian.[47] Piper uses this verse in his evangelistic tract[48] and pleads with those searching to call upon God's name for salvation.[49] Matthew 5:44 shows God's love toward the world in perhaps the greatest way. Christ commands the Christian to love his enemies. He states those who love only friends are no better than unbelievers.[50] Only someone with the heart of God loves his enemies.[51] Loving enemies means doing good to them in the same way God does good to them; helping them with the ordinary things of life; purposely doing good to them; and sharing Christ with them.[52]

The revealed will, universal love, missions, and Christian Hedonism connect in other ways. God in Scripture promises that one day people from all people groups will worship before the throne. Regarding sharing the gospel in general and missions in particular,

---

47   John Piper, "Strengthened to Suffer: Christ, Noah, and Baptism," <http://www.desiringgod.org/library/sermons/94/092594.html>, site editor, Desiring God Ministries, September 25, 1994, accessed on 21 November 2004; John Piper, "What Answers Do Prayers Depend on?: Part2, <http://www.desiringgod.org/library/ sermons/81/012581.html>, site editor, Desiring God Ministries, January 25, 1981, accessed on 21 November 2004; and John Piper, "What Is Baptism and Does it Save?," <http://www.desiringgod.org/library/sermons/97/051897.html>, site editor, Desiring God Ministries, May 18, 1997, accessed on 21 November 2004.

48   Piper, "Quest for Joy."

49   John Piper, "Thanks Be to God for His Inexpressible Gift," <http://www. desiringgod.org/library/sermons/89/111989.html>, site editor, Desiring God Ministries, November 19, 1989, accessed on 21 November 2004; John Piper, "Joy Recovered," <http://www.desiringgod.org/library/sermons/89/021289.html>, site editor, Desiring God Ministries, February 12, 1989, accessed on 21 November 2004; and John Piper, "God's Invincible Purpose Part Five: Foundations for Full Assurance: God Called Us into Life and Hope," <http://www.desiringgod.org/ library/ sermons/92/040592.html>, site editor, Desiring God Ministries, April 5, 1992, accessed on 21 November 2004.

50   Piper, "Doing Mercy to the Brothers of Jesus and the Broken Neighbor."

51   Piper, "The Greatest of These Is Love: But I Say to You, Love Your Enemies Part One."

52   Piper, "The Greatest of These Is Love: Love Your Neighbor as Yourself Part Two."

Scripture reveals that the Christian is God's example to the world. The Christian has the responsibility to share Christ.[53] Acting kind to the lost and doing good works serves as a witnessing tool (Matt 5:16).[54] The Golden Rule, for instance, not only commands the Christian to act kindly, but also it is a witness of God's love to the unregenerate.[55] Christ's command to love one's neighbor as

---

53   John Piper, "Good Deeds and the Glory of God," <http://www.desiring-god.org/library/sermons/87/021587p.html>, site editor, Desiring God Ministries, February 15, 1987, accessed on November 20, 2004. See also: John Piper, "What Jesus Did After the Beginning," <http://www.desiringgod.org/library/sermons/90/ 091690.html>, site editor, Desiring God Ministries, September 16, 1990, accessed on November 29, 2004; John Piper, "Doing Mercy to Brothers of Jesus and the Broken Hearted," <http://www.desiring god.org/library/sermons/ 04/100304.html>, site editor, Desiring God Ministries, October 3, 2004, accessed on November 29, 2004; John Piper, "Christ, Culture and Abortion," <http://www. desiringgod.org/library/sermons/00/122300.html>, site editor, Desiring God Ministries, December 23, 2000, accessed on November 29, 2004; John Piper, "The Local Church: Minimum Vs Maximum," <http://www. desiringgod.org/library/sermons/ 81/032981.html>, site editor, Desiring God Ministries, March 29, 1981, accessed on 21 November 2004; John Piper, "Prayer: The Work of Missions;" <http://desiringgod.org/library/sermons/96/122996.html>, site editor, Desiring God Ministries, December 29, 1996, accessed 19 January 2004; and Piper, "Heart's Desire."

54   John Piper, "O Be Not Mere Shadows, Echoes, and Residue," <http://www.desiringgod.org/library/fresh_words/1999/100599.html>, site editor, Desiring God Ministries, October 5, 1999, accessed on November 20, 2004; John Piper, "Peculiar Doctrines, Public Morals, and the Political Welfare: Reflections on the Life and Labor of William Wilberforce," <http://desiringgod.org/library/biographies/02wilberforce.html>, site editor, Desiring God Ministries, February 5, 2002, accessed on November 20, 2004; Piper, "Good Deeds and the Glory of God;" and John Piper, "How to Do Good So God Gets the Glory," <http://www.desiring god.org/library/sermons/80/080380.html>, site editor, Desiring God Ministries, August 3, 1980, accessed on November 20, 2004; and Piper, "The Greatest of These Is Love: But I Say to You, Love Your Enemies Part One.

55   John Piper, "The Greatest of These Is Love: Love Your Neighbor as Yourself Part Two," <http://www.desiringgod.org/library/sermons/95/050795.html>, site editor, Desiring God Ministries, May 7,

oneself (Matt 22:34–40) is another example. Christ desires the Christian to pursue sharing the gospel with the non-Christian in the same way the Christian pursues love for God. In this way, Christians represent a loving God to the world. Piper explains this must be done with the same motivation: "Jesus is not just saying: seek for your neighbor the same things you seek for yourself, but also seek them in the same way—the same zeal and energy and creativity and perseverance."[56]

Acts 1:8 and Matt 28:18–20 demonstrate that witnessing is more than being kind; it involves sharing the gospel. God has given Christians the power to proclaim Christ to all people groups.[57] Matthew 28:18–20 also commands the Christian to go to all people groups and present the gospel. Piper stresses that the Great Commission applies for people of all ages; it was not given just to the apostles.[58] All Christians are responsible to proclaim the message of Christ to all peoples:

1995, accessed on 8 November 2004. See also: John Piper, "The Greatest of These Is Love: But I Say to You, Love Your Enemies Part One," <http://www.desiringgod.org/library/sermons/95/051495.html>, site editor, Desiring God Ministries, May 14, 1995, accessed on 8 November 2004.

56   Piper, "The Greatest of These Is Love: Love Your Neighbor as Yourself Part Two. See also: Piper, "The Greatest of These Is Love: But I Say to You, Love Your Enemies Part One," italics his.

57   John Piper, "You Shall Receive Power Till Jesus Comes," <http://www. desiringgod.org/library/sermons/90/093090.html>, site editor, Desiring God Ministries, September 30, 1990, accessed on 22 November 2004 and John Piper, "The Lofty Claim, the Last Command, the Loving Comfort," <http://www.desiring god.org/library/sermons/98/110198. html>, site editor, Desiring God Ministries, November 1, 1998, accessed on 22 November 2004. See also: Piper, "The Spirit Wants the World for Christ;" Piper, "The Price and the Preciousness of Spiritual Power," Piper, "Old and Young Shall Dream Together;" and Piper, "That All the Nations Might Hear.

58   John Piper, "Go and Make Disciples Baptizing Them," <http://www. desiringgod.org/library/sermons/82/111482.html>, site editor, Desiring God Ministries, November 14, 1982, accessed 22 November 2004.

There is not a culture or an ethnic group or a society or a religion or a language where Jesus does not have the right to be worshiped as Lord. He has authority to be king and Lord and Savior everywhere, to everyone. This is the reason he commands us to make disciples in all the peoples of the world. . . . Jesus Christ, the living, all-authoritative Lord of the universe, has commanded us to call every nation, every people (Somali, Maninka, Sukumu) and every religion (Muslim, Buddhist, Hindu, animist) to repent and believe in Jesus for the forgiveness of sins and the inheritance of eternal life with the one true God.[59]

Piper exhorts the Christian to share the gospel as a means of thankfulness. He asks, "How can we feel the wonder of having been rescued freely by Christ, and then not live for the rescue of others?"[60] Piper suggests several ways the Christian can foster an attitude of desire for the lost:

1. the Christian should be reminded those without Christ spend eternity in hell
2. Christ's death is powerful enough to save every person
3. God can turn even the hardest heart to him
4. there is tremendous joy in heaven when a person converts
5. remember that one's own salvation is completely by the grace of God
6. act on the love that is already in the heart
7. pray that God would increase a passion for the lost in one's heart.[61]

---

59 Piper, "The Lofty Claim, the Last Command, the Loving Comfort." See also: John Piper, "Worship the Risen Christ," <http://www.desiringgod.org/library/sermons/ 83/040383. html>, site editor, Desiring God Ministries, April 3,1983, accessed on 22 November 2004; and Piper, "Go and Make Disciples, Baptizing Them."
60 Piper, "Heart's Desire."
61 Ibid.

THE SECRET WILL, GOD'S ELECTING LOVE, AND
MISSIONS

As God finds joy in his universal love, he finds joy in election. Since God's joy is the foundation for Christian Hedonism, whatever he does pleases him, including in electing people to salvation. When God chose Israel to be his people, he elected her with gladness apart from her works. According to Deut 10:14–15 and 7:5–6, God's election of Israel was from grace.[62] Luke 10:21, one of two passages in the Gospels where Christ is said to rejoice,[63] explains that Christ rejoices that God hides salvation from the wise and gives it to those poor in understanding, implying the free and unconditional nature of God's electing love.[64]

Christian Hedonism's concept of conversion is part of God's secret will as it is part of his revealed will. While God desires salvation for every person, his electing love saves only his children.[65] Electing love is God's unconditional election. God loves his children with a love that is different than his love for humankind in general.[66] Piper compares the universal love of God with the electing love of God using an illustration of man's love for his wife compared to his love for other women:

> God loves the world—such that he gave his only begotten Son that whosoever believes on him shall not perish

---

62 Piper, *The Pleasures of God*, 128–33.
63 Piper, *The Pleasures of God*, 134.
64 Ibid., 135.
65 John Piper, "I am God Almighty, Be Fruitful and Multiply: I Have Other Sheep," <http://www.desiringgod.org/library/sermons/96/030396. html>, site editor, Desiring God Ministries, March 3, 1996, accessed on 4 December 2004.
66 John Piper, "God Has Given Us Good Hope Through Grace," <http:// www.desiringgod.org/library/sermons/87/090687.html>, site editor, Desiring God Ministries, September 6, 1987, accessed on 2 December 2004. See also: John Piper, "Do Not Harden Your Heart in the Day of Trial," <http://www.desiringgod.org/library/sermons/96/081196.html>, site editor, Desiring God Ministries, August 11, 1996, accessed on 02 December 2004.

but have everlasting life (John 3:16). But it is a great sad-
ness when a wife only knows herself loved with the love
that her husband has for every woman. The marriage
between Christ and his wife is weak—and the church is
weak—to the degree that she only feels loved with the
same love that allows others in the world to perish, as
though there were no peculiar love that chose her and
raised her to life and made a covenant with her never to
turn away from doing her good.[67]

Piper believes the free and unconditional nature of the
doctrine of election shows that God elects solely for his purposes,
apart from any work of the person converted. The impossibility of
missions without the power of the Holy Spirit (through the proclamation of the gospel) to save the elect should evoke hope in the
Christian[68] because the success of missions depends on God and
not the Christian.[69] Piper explains:

If God were not in charge in this affair doing the hu-
manly impossible, the missionary task would be hope-
less. Who but God can raise the spiritually dead and give
them an ear for the gospel (Acts 16:14)? The great Biblical doctrines of unconditional election, and predestination unto sonship, and irresistible grace in the preaching
of Christ are mighty incentives.[70]

---

67 John Piper, "Beautifying the Body of Christ," <http://www.desiringgod.
   org/ library/sermons/92/101192.html>, site editor, Desiring God Ministries, October 11, 1992, accessed on 2 December 2004.

68 John Piper, "The Fruit of Hope: Boldness," <http://www.desiringgod.org/
   library/sermons/86/072086.html>, site editor, Desiring God Ministries,
   July 20, 1986, accessed on 31 December 2004. See also: Piper, "Those
   Whom He Predestined He Also Called: Part One;" and Piper, "Those
   Whom He Predestined He Also Called: Part Two."

69 John Piper, "A Pastor's Role in World Missions;" <http://www.desiring
   god.org/library/topics/pastors_role.html>, site editor, Desiring God
   Ministries, accessed 03 March 2004

70 John Piper, "Missions: The Battle Cry of Christian Hedonism," <http://
   www.desiringgod.org/library/sermons/83/111383.html>, site editor, De-

Deuteronomy 29:29 implies that certain things belong to God's secret will; "mysteries" for God to know alone.[71] Piper contends that one of the "mysteries," election, is part of the secret will when he discusses Jeremiah's call to salvation and ministry. When Jeremiah fears his calling, God states that he predestined him for this work. As Jeremiah's ministry and election are "rooted in the unshakable, sovereign purposes of God,"[72] the Christians' are as well. Ephesians 1:4 states God predestined the Christian before the foundation of the world,[73] apart from a person's knowledge and work. Romans 8:28 states that all things work together for good for those who love God and are "called according to [God's] purpose." Those who are called are the elect; God's purpose is his secret will.[74] Second Timothy 1:9 states that God elected the Christian for God's own purpose. God, from eternity "willed to pass on his 'eternal inheritance'" to his elect.[75] Ephesians 1:11

siring God Ministries, November 13, 1983, accessed on 30 December 2004.

71   John Piper, "Pastor Thoughts on the Doctrine of Election," <http://www. desiringgod.org/library/sermons/03/113003.html>, site editor, Desiring God Ministries, November 30, 2003, accessed on 21 December 2004.

72   John Piper, "Do Not Say 'I am Only a Youth,'" <http://www.desiringgod. org/ library/sermons/89/090389.html>, site editor, Desiring God Ministries, September 9, 1989, accessed on 21 December 2004.

73   John Piper, "God's Invincible Purpose: Part One: Foundations for Full Assurance," <http://www.desiringgod.org/library/sermons/92/030192. html>, site editor, Desiring God Ministries, March 1, 1992, accessed on 21 December 2004.

74   John Piper, "Called According to His Purpose," <http://www.desiring-god.org/ library/sermons/85/101385.html>, site editor, Desiring God Ministries, October 13, 1985, accessed on 21 December 2004. See also: Piper, "Those Whom He Predestined He Also Called: Part One."

75   John Piper, "How the Called Receive An Eternal Inheritance," <http:// www.desiringgod.org/library/sermons/97/012697.html>, site editor, Desiring God Ministries, January 26, 1997, accessed on 21 December 2004. See also: John Piper, "Why Hope Grace!," <http://www.desiring-god.org/library/sermons/86/ 041386.html>, site editor, Desiring God Ministries, April 13, 1992, accessed on 21 December 2004; John Piper, "God's Word Stands: Christ Came to Confirm It," <http://www.desiring god.org/library/sermons/02/122202html>, site editor, Desiring God

states that God elected Jacob over Esau before birth, before they could commit good works, and God accomplishes all things according to his will. In Question 11 of, "A Baptist Catechism," Piper asks, "What are the decrees of God?" The reply: "The decrees of God are his eternal purpose, according to the counsel of his will, whereby for his own glory, he has foreordained whatsoever comes to pass," including election. Ephesians 1:11 is used as a reference.[76] Perhaps the most significant passage that connects the secret will with election is Rom 9:11. Just as God chose Jacob over Esau before they sinned,[77] a Christian can take no credit for conversion.[78] Piper stresses this idea when he states, "The point

---

Ministries, December 22, 2002, accessed on 21 December 2004; and John Piper, "The God-Centered Ground for Saving Grace: Grace Upon Grace: The Incomparable Riches of God," <http://www.desiringgod.org/ library/topics/gods_passion/god_centered_groundhtml>, site editor, Desiring God Ministries, March 25, 1995, accessed on 21 December 2004.

76   John Piper, "A Baptist Catechism: (Adapted By John Piper)," <http:// www.desiringgod.org/library/what_we_believe/catechism.html>, site editor, Desiring God Ministries, accessed on 21 December 2004. See also: John Piper, "All Things are From God, Through God, and To God. The Glory is All His," <http://www.desiring god.org/library/sermons/04/032804.html>, site editor, Desiring God Ministries, March 28, 2004, accessed on 21 December 2004.

77   Piper, "Called According to His Purpose."

78   John Piper, "The Argument of Romans 9:14–16," <http://www.desiringgod.org/library/topics/doctrines_grace/romans_9.html>, site editor, Desiring God Ministries, March 1976, accessed on 21 December 2004; John Piper, "The Absolute Sovereignty of God: What is Romans Nine About," <http://www.desiringgod. org/library/sermons/02/110302. html>, site editor, Desiring God Ministries, November 3, 2002, accessed on 21 December 2004; John Piper, "The Fame of His Name and the Freedom of His Mercy," <http://www.desiringgod.org/library/ sermons/03/020203.html>, site editor, Desiring God Ministries, February 2, 2003, accessed on 21 December 2004; John Piper, "For God's Sake, Let Grace Be Grace," <http://www.desiring god.org/ library/sermons/03/111603.html>, site editor, Desiring God Ministries, November 16, 2003, accessed on 21 December 2004; and John Piper, "Boasting in Man is Doubly Excluded," <http://www.desiringgod.org/ library/ fresh_words/2003/ 030503.html>, site editor, Desiring God Ministries,

is that his [God's] choices in determining which vessels or which persons serve which ends are based on his own secret wisdom, not on the free choices of men."[79] The connection between the secret will and election is reiterated when placed within the context of the sovereignty of God. In, "What the Pastoral Staff of Bethlehem Baptist Church Emphasize in Their Teaching," the relationship is apparent:

> The God of the Bible is the creator of the whole visible and invisible universe and He is the sovereign ruler of it. From all eternity, He freely and unchangeably, in His most holy wisdom, ordained whatsoever comes to pass. To use the words of Paul, God does "all things according to the counsel of His will" (Ephesians 1:11), having sovereign control of all events from the events of rulers and nations (Daniel 4:25, 32, 34–35) to the flight of a sparrow (Matthew 10:29). In particular, Gods sovereignty is worked out in the area of salvation. To ensure that the salvation of sinners abounds to the praise of God's glory, God saves His people by grace alone apart from works, lest anyone should boast (Ephesians 2:8– 9). The sovereignty of God's grace is seen in God's unconditional election of His people out of the mass of sinful humanity for salvation (Romans 8:29, 9:6-23; Ephesians 1:4), the glorious atonement of Christ which actually accomplishes the salvation of God's people (I Peter 3:18), the irresistible grace of God's effectual call (Romans 8:30; I Peter 2:9) and the regenerating work of the Holy Spirit (Jeremiah 31:31-34; Ezekiel 36:26ff, John 3:4; Titus 3:5) which enable and move a person to respond to the gospel of Christ in saving faith, and God's persevering in grace with his saints (I Peter 1:5; Jude 1; John 10:28-30;

March 5, 2003, accessed on 21 December 2004.

79   Piper, *The Justification of God*, 197.

Philippians 1:6) so that His people will in fact persevere to the end and be saved.[80]

Regarding the secret will and missions, Piper asserts the beginning of the Protestant Modern Missions Movement was impacted positively by those who promoted the Reformed doctrine of predestination. The connection between election and missions is alive among contemporary missionaries as well. Piper cites David and Faith Jaegar, missionaries to Liberia, who state that trusting in the sovereignty of God is more important than any type of preparation.[81] Piper quotes John Alexander, formerly head of InterVarsity Christian Fellowship who credits being a missionary with changing his position on election: "[A]fter years in the field I say, 'If predestination is not true I could never be a missionary.'"[82]

The connection between God's electing love and missions is a theme in many of Piper's works, especially his sermons and talks.[83] The clearest connection between election and missions is John 10, which explains that there are some sheep who are Christ's and others who are not. The ones who are Christ's have been given to him by the Father. When Christ's calls them they will respond. They will respond because they are his sheep, not vice-versa. Piper makes this point clear: "being one of Christ's sheep enables you to respond to his call. It is not the other way around: responding

---

80   "What the Pastoral Staff of Bethlehem Baptist Church Emphasize in Their Teaching," <http://www.desiringgod.org/library/what_we_believe/pastoral_ teaching.html>, site editor, Desiring God Ministries, accessed on 21 December 2004.

81   John Piper, "Hallowed Be Thy Name: In All the Earth," <http://www.desiringgod.org/library/sermons/84/110484.html>, site editor, Desiring God Ministries, November 4, 1984, accessed on 1 January 2005.

82   Piper, "Missions: The Battle Cry of Christian Hedonism."

83   For example: Piper, "For God's Sake, Let Grace Be Grace;" Piper, "Called According to His Purpose;" John Piper, "I Am the Lord, and Besides Me There Is No Savior: Education for Exultation: In God," <http://www.desiringgod.org/library/sermons/00/ 013000.html>, site editor, Desiring God Ministries, January 30, 2000, accessed on 4 January 2005; Piper, "Pastoral Thoughts on the Doctrine of Election;"

to his call does not make you one of his sheep."[84] Piper considers
John 10:16, "I have other sheep that are not of this fold; I must
bring them also," the "GREAT missionary text" in John[85] and the
"battle cry" of missions.[86] He believes John 10:16 (and similar
passages such as Acts 18:10, John 11:52; and 17:20) makes the
task of missions definite[87] and should serve to inspire missionaries.[88] Piper gives four reasons why John 10:16 should bring hope
to the missionaries. First, there are others besides those who are already saved that God intends to save.[89] Second, the passage shows
God intends to save some who are presently unregenerate that are
outside the fold of Israel.[90] The term "other sheep" combined with
Rev 5:9 implies there are people throughout the whole world who
God will save. Since God promises to save them, his will will be
accomplished.[91] Third, God will elect using the Christian to proclaim the gospel. God not only ordains the means (election) but

---

84   Piper, "I Have Other Sheep That are Not of This Fold." See also: Piper,
      Desiring God, 236–40.

85   Ibid. Emphasis his.

86   Piper, "A Baptist Catechism."

87   Piper, "I Have Sheep That are Not of This Fold."

88   Piper, "Those Whom He Predestined He Also Called: Part Two." See
      also: John Piper, "Ten Effects of Believing in the Five Points of Cal-
      vinism," <http://www. desiringgod.org/library/topics/doctrine_grace/
      ten_effects.html>, site editor, Desiring God Ministries, April 20, 2002,
      accessed on 4 January 2005; Piper, *Desiring God*, 236–38.

89   Piper, "I Have Other Sheep That are Not of This Fold" and Piper, "I am
      God Almighty, Be Fruitful and Multiply." See also: Piper, *Desiring God*,
      236–40.

90   John Piper, "The Hour Has Come for the Son of Man to Be Glorified,"
      <http://www.desiringgod.org/library/sermons/85/033185.html>, site
      editor, Desiring God Ministries, April 20, 2002, accessed on 4 January
      2005. See also: Piper, "I Have Other Sheep That are Not of This Fold;"
      Piper, "I am God Almighty, Be Fruitful and Multiply;" and Piper, *Desir-
      ing God*, 236–40.

91   Piper, "What We Believe About the Five Points of Calvinism." See also:
      John Piper, "You Have Filled Jerusalem with Your Teaching," <http://
      www.desiringgod.org/ library/sermons/91/030391>, site editor, Desiring
      God Ministries, March 3, 1991, accessed on 4 January 2005.

also the method (the proclamation of the gospel). Piper does not advocate the Hyper-Calvinist notion that God will save without using the Christian to preach the good news.[92] Fourth, Christ's sheep will respond. Some may resist him longer, but if they are part of the elect, they will answer his effectual call.[93]

Piper responds to the question, "Why share the gospel, if only the elect are saved? The answer falls under the secret will of God. Part of the justification of God is to elect in his divine sovereignty some for salvation and others for damnation.[94] However, Piper sees similarities to God's impartiality with Jews and Greeks. Both Jews and Greeks are guilty before God because of their sin. Judgment is based on acting upon the knowledge one has, and all have the moral law of God in their hearts: all know they have been created by God, are reliant upon God, should worship God, and failure to do this results in death.[95] This idea is similar to those who die with no knowledge of the gospel: they failed to glorify and worship God despite having knowledge about God through general revelation. He concludes, "God is not unjust. No one will ever be condemned for not believing a message he has never heard. Those who have never heard the gospel will be judged by their failure to own up to the light of God's grace and power in nature and in their own conscience."[96]

Another aspect of Christian Hedonism that connects God's secret will and his electing love with missions is suffering, or more generally, evil. Piper separates evil into two categories, natural and moral evil. Natural evil is things like cancer and tornadoes; moral evil is sinful action. Scripture demonstrates that God is sovereign

---

92 Piper, "I Have Other Sheep That are Not of This Fold;" and Piper, "I am God Almighty, Be Fruitful and Multiply."

93 Ibid.

94 Piper, *The Justification of God*, 101.

95 Piper, "There is No Partially with God." See also: John Piper, "There is No Partially with God [Part Two]," <http://www.desiringgod.org/library/sermons/99/ 013199.html>, site editor, Desiring God Ministries, January 31, 1999, accessed on 10 January 2005.

96 Piper, *Desiring God*, 227.

over natural evil. Passages such as Job 1:21–22, Deut 32:39, 2 Sam 12:15, and 1 Sam 2:6–7 testify God controls life and death. Other passages such as Ex 4:11 and 1 Pet 3:17 state God controls disease and suffering. However, God may will the Christian to suffer. Job 2:10 states while Job is afflicted with sores, he comments that one should accept the good as well as the evil things from God.[97] God is also in control over moral evil. Piper states, "God purposely governs the sinful choices of people."[98] This does not mean Piper believes God originated sin. God does not sin, nor is he the instrument of sin; God permits sin to exist. This is not because God enjoys evil; instead, he "wills evil come to pass . . . that good may come out of it."[99] In connecting suffering with missions, the secret will of God and election, Piper states that the glory of God is paramount:

> The ultimate purpose of the universe is to display the greatness of the glory of the grace of God. The highest, clearest, surest display of that glory is in the suffering of the best Person in the universe for millions of undeserving sinners. Therefore, the ultimate reason that suffering exists in the universe is so that Christ might display the greatness of the glory of the grace of God by suffering in himself to overcome our suffering and bring about the praise of the glory of the grace of God."[100]

---

97   Piper, "Is God Less Glorious Because He Ordained that Evil Be?"
98   Ibid.
99   Ibid.
100 John Piper, "The Suffering of Christ and the Sovereignty of God,"
     <http://www.desiringgod.org/ResourceLibrary/ConferenceMessages/
     ByConference/1/228_The_Suffering_of_Christ_and_the_Sovereign-
     ty_of_God/>, site editor, Desiring God Ministries, October 9, 2005,
     accessed 5 February 2010.

GOD'S GLORY SEEN IN THE TWO WILLS OF GOD THESIS AS THE MOTIVATION FOR PIPER'S MISSIOLOGY

Revealed Will

In God's revealed will, creation, human government, and human consciousness connect God's glory and common grace.[101] The fundamental reason God finds joy in creation is because it manifests his glory.[102] Creation points people to God. God gives every person an opportunity to experience him and seek after him. No one has reason to reject him.[103] Regarding common grace, Piper asks, "Is it not possible that what Paul means in Rom 2:4 is that in the interval of life given to men and nations, everything in (Rom 1:18–23; Acts 14:17) and history (Acts 17:26f) and the human conscience (Rom 2:5) is pointing (i.e. "leading") men to repentance and faith?"[104] Humankind was supposed to be fruitful and multiply and fill the earth in order that the "knowledge of God's glory would cover the sea."[105] Piper implies the conscience of the unbeliever glorifies God when he treats others fairly.[106]

Piper's understanding of Christian Hedonism further promotes the connection between God's revealed will and his glory. This can be seen in the phrase, "God is most glorified in us when

101 Piper, "The Pleasure of God in His Creation."

102 Ibid.

103 Piper, *Let the Nations Be Glad!*, 192 n 34, realizes that babies who die and those with severe mental defects cannot experience general revelation. In these cases, Piper believes they go to heaven when they die. For more information see: "What Happens to Infants When They Die," <http://www.desiringgod.org/library/theological_qa/infant_salv/infants html>, site editor, Desiring God Ministries, accessed on 13 November 2004.

104 Piper, *The Justification of God*, 208.

105 John Piper, "God Created Us for His Glory," <http://www.desiringgod.org/ library/sermons/80/072780.html>, site editor, Desiring God Ministries, July 27, 1980, accessed on 12 January 2005.

106 John Piper, "The Pleasure of God in Public Justice," <http://www.desiringgod. org/library/sermons/87/040587.html>, site editor, Desiring God Ministries, April 5, 1987, accessed on 12 January 2005.

we are most satisfied in him." Piper explains that loving someone in a God-honoring manner is a:

> humble, sacrificial, self-giving interaction that helps people treasure Christ above all things. In other words, love seeks, at whatever cost, to spread into the heart of the beloved a joyful passion for God's supreme value in all things through Jesus Christ. People are most loved not when they are made much of, but when they are helped to enjoy making much of God forever.[107]

The revealed will of God demonstrates that God loves universally. God demonstrates his universal love through his commandments and promises. Two commandments, the charge to love God and the charge to love one another, are intrinsically related, and when obeyed, present a tangible display of God's universal love for the world.[108] Piper's understanding of common grace and Christian Hedonism promote God's love for the world. God loves in the same way he commands people to love. God commands humans to be kind to all; and he is kind to all.[109] God commands Christians to call humankind to repentance; and he calls all humankind to repentance.[110] God commands that Christians do good works in order that people glorify him; and he does good works for the same reason. God commands love for enemies; God

---

107 John Piper, "Doing Mercy to the Brothers of Jesus and the Broken Neighbor," <http://www.desiringgod.org/library/sermons/04/100304. html>, site editor, Desiring God Ministries, October 3, 2004, accessed on 22 November 2004. See also John Piper, "The Mission and Vision of Bethlehem Baptist Church: Volume Two: A Passion for the Supremacy of God for the Joy of All Peoples Unpacking the Master Planning Team Document," <http://www.desiringgod.org/library/sermons/95/ 100195. html>, site editor, Desiring God Ministries, October 1, 1995, accessed on 22 November 2004.

108 Piper, "The Greatest of These is Love: Love Your Neighbor as You Love Yourself: Part One."

109 Piper, "How Does a Sovereign God Love."

110 Ibid.

loves his enemies.[111] God commands people to be happy in him; and God is happy in himself.[112] No one deserves the provisions of God's universal love, but God gives them to all.[113] God could have destroyed humankind long before, but because God loves he suffered through their disobedience and refusal to repent with the intent that some would come to Christ and magnify his glory.[114] Honoring the glory of God, being fulfilled in him, and treasuring him above all things evidences God's love for the world.[115]

Secret Will

The secret will of God brings God glory through election. The doctrine of election should evoke joy in the Christian and enable him to praise God's glory.[116] These connection between Piper's understanding of the doctrine of election and God's glory is best seen in his interpretation of Rom 9:11–16. Piper believes this passage promotes unconditional, individual election and reprobation to the glory of God.[117] Romans 9:11 shows that if God did not elect unconditionally he would fail to be glorious because God's glory is intrinsically bound to his freedom and sovereignty.

111 Ibid.

112 Piper, *Desiring God*, 17; 31–52.

113 John Piper, "God Works for Those Who Wait for Him," <http://www.desiringgod.org/library/sermons/82/090582.html>, site editor, Desiring God Ministries, September 5, 1982, accessed 01 November 2004.

114 John Piper, "God's Response to Hypocrisy: Kindness and Judgement," <http://www.desiringgod.org/library/sermons/98/112298.html>, site editor, Desiring God Ministries, November 11, 1998, accessed on 9 November 2004.

115 John Piper, "Worship Is an End in Itself," <http://desiringgod.org/library/ sermons/81/091381.html>, site editor, Desiring God Ministries, September 13, 1981, accessed on 09 January 2004; and John Piper, "A Response to Richard Mouw's Treatment of Christian Hedonism in The God Who Commands," <http//www.desiringgod.org/library/topics/ christian_hedonism/mouw.html>, site editor, Desiring God Ministries, accessed 08 January 2004.

116 Piper, "The Freedom and Justice of God in Unconditional Election."

117 Piper makes the point clear in *The Justification of God*, a book that is an exegetical and theological analysis of Rom 9:1–23.

God's election is "not based on [human] deeds in any way: not deeds already done, not deeds undone and foreknown, and not deeds undone and not foreknown. [God's] election is free. That is [his] glory."[118] The phrase in Ex 33:19, "I will have mercy on whom I have mercy, and I will have compassion on whom I have compassion," the same phrase used in Rom 9:15, is important to this connection. Taken within the context of Ex 33:12–34:9, two concurrent themes occupy the passage: Moses' prayer that God would guide Israel to the promised land and Moses' prayer to see God's glory.[119] The request to see God's glory is answered when God, based on God's "free and sovereign choice,"[120] shows favor to a "stiffnecked, idolatrous people" (Ex 33:16–17). Piper concludes, based on Ex 33:19, that there is an inextricable connection between God's glory and election.[121] Romans 9:14–15 gives the same meaning. Piper states, "God's name, the essence of his glory, consists in his absolute freedom to have mercy on whom he will have mercy."[122]

The secret will of God demonstrates that he loves the elect effectually. God finds joy in his electing love, and Scripture indicates the doctrine of election is something to cherish. While this type of love is different than the type of love God commands for Christians to share with the unsaved, electing love does not negate the responsibility Christians have in the proclamation of the gospel cross-culturally. Piper notes Christians are the only ones able

---

118 Ibid.

119 John Piper, "Prolegomena to Understanding Romans 9:4–15: An Interpretation of Exodus 33:19," *Journal of the Evangelical Theological Society*, 22, no. 3 (September 1979): 207; John Piper, "I Will Be Gracious To Whom I Will Be Gracious," <http://www.desiring god.org/library/sermons/84/092384.html>, site editor, Desiring God Ministries, September 23, 1984, accessed on 12 January 2005; and Piper, *The Justification of God*, 75–89.

120 Piper, *The Justification of God*, 79–83; 208–11; Piper, "I Will Be Gracious To Whom I Will Be Gracious."

121 Piper, "I Will Be Gracious To Whom I Will Be Gracious;" and Piper, *The Justification of God*, 88–89; 215.

122 Piper, "The Freedom and Justice of God in Unconditional Election."

to fulfill the commandments to love God and others completely because the unregenerate have no desire or ability. The lost are without God's grace being totally depraved, having a sinful heart toward God and all godly things. [123]

GOD'S GLORY MOTIVATES PIPER'S MISSIOLOGY

Piper believes the revealed and secret wills of God are each "an effort to say yes to the universal, saving will of 1 Timothy 2:4 and yes to the individual, unconditional election of Romans 9:6–23."[124] The revealed will of God shows God's universal love for all people, and the secret will of God shows God's effectual love for the elect. Piper states while a promotion of the Two Wills of God Thesis may be illogical and difficult for people to understand or reconcile, it is quite biblical and exegetically sound.[125] He states a "simultaneous existence of God's will for 'all men to be saved' (1 Timothy 2:4) and his will to elect unconditionally those who will actually be saved is not a sign of divine schizophrenia or exegetical confusion;"[126] it is a sign of the magnificence of God's glory.[127]

Piper's interpretations of biblical passages connect God's glory, the will of God, and missions. The quintessential passage is Romans 9. Piper took a sabbatical from Bethel College to research and understand its meaning.[128] It not only led him to resign his position from Bethel and become pastor of Bethlehem Baptist Church, but he also came away with an understanding that God's

---

123 Piper, "What We Believe About the Five Points of Calvinism."

124 Piper, *The Pleasures of God*, 331.

125 Ibid., 313.

126 Piper, The Pleasures of God, 313. See also: John Piper, "How Shall People Be Saved: Part Two," <http://www.desiring god.org/library/sermons/03/ 083103.html>, site editor, Desiring God Ministries, August 31, 2003, accessed on 22 January 2005.

127 Piper, *The Pleasures of God*, 313–40. These pages deal with how this issue relates to God's glory.

128 Piper, "The Absolute Sovereignty of God." This is when *The Justification of God* was written.

purpose for humankind is to "see and savor and sing—and spread a passion for—the glory of God"[129] in order that "his name be declared in all the earth."[130]

---

129 Piper, "Unconditional Election And the Invincible Purpose of God."
130 Piper, *The Justification of God*, 170.

10

CONCLUSION

Piper provides a way forward for Christians interested in missions who want a theologically Calvinist rationale. Piper also gives non-Calvinists justification for their critique of Calvinists who do not engage in cross-cultural evangelism. Piper believes everything God does is for his glory. God created the universe, works in history, and sent Christ to redeem humankind all for his glory. God saves in order that people will worship him. Worship requires being happy in God, because "God is most glorified in us when we are most satisfied in him." This is the essence of Christian Hedonism. A central facet of Christian Hedonism is sharing the gospel cross-culturally with peoples who have not heard of Christ. This type of missions gives God glory because it brings "glad-hearted worshipers" into the kingdom from all people groups. Piper's understanding of God's glory, seen through his understanding of the Two Wills of God Thesis, motivates his missiology. It also reconciles how one person contradicts a belief that Calvinist theology and missions and evangelism are irreconcilable. There is no salvation apart from the proclamation of the gospel and God elects who he chooses; therefore, Christians should find sharing their faith a joy because it shows God is using them to conduct his divine plan.[1] While Piper is not without flaws, he is one of the few Christian personalities who has been in ministry for decades but has not sullied his faith or made a mockery of the gospel. Regardless of their theological system, Christians can see his example and

---

1   John Piper, "Those Whom He Predestined He Also Called," <http://www.desiringgod.org/library/sermons/85/102085.html>, site editor, Desiring God Ministries, October 20, 1985, accessed on 09 February 2004.

model it to reach the nations for Christ. This chapter will address questions answered and unanswered by this book.

QUESTIONS ANSWERED AND UNANSWERED

Questions Answered

In this work I answered the following questions concerning Piper:1) Who influenced Piper's thought? 2) What is Piper's understanding of theology and is it orthodox? 3) What is Piper's understanding of missions? 4) How does Piper's understanding of Calvinism relate to his promotion of missions? 5) How does Piper's understanding of the glory of God motivate his missiology?

Piper's understanding of the revealed and secret wills of God falls within traditional, conservative, evangelical thought. His understanding of the two wills of God is neither Calvinist nor Arminian, though he himself is a Calvinist. Calvinists and non-Calvinists alike promote distinctions in the will of God and maintain that the wills are interrelated. Both the Calvinist and the non-Calvinist might agree with apologist John Frame who states the distinction between God's secret will and his revealed will this way:

> [t]he former governs whatever comes to pass; the latter expresses what God wants us to believe and to do. The former is secret until it is carried out in history; we cannot use it to predict the future. Nor can we use it alone to direct our lives; for such direction, God has given us the perceptive [revealed] will in the Scriptures.[2]

The difference between Calvinist and non-Calvinist, Piper states, is a matter of emphasis. Calvinists focus on the glory of God in election; non-Calvinists center on the freedom of humankind to choose Christ in salvation.[3]

---

2   John Frame, *Apologetics for the Glory of God: An Introduction* (Phillips-burg, PA: Presbyterian & Reformed, 1994), 175 n 5.

3   John Piper, *The Pleasures of God: Meditations on God's Delight in Being God*, rev. and expanded ed. (Sisters, OR: Multnomah, 2000), 333–34.

I also showed in this work that one cannot state unequivocally that Calvinism hinders missions, as some suggest.[4] Some of the most popular and influential missionaries and missions minded people are Calvinists. Piper himself states that Christians cannot be "true Calvinist[s]" unless they are missions minded.[5]

In this book I showed the importance of Piper's understanding of God's glory. God's glory is seen in his theology and missiology. In his missiology, Piper desires to see God save people from every people group for the purpose of worship. His understanding of God's glory relates to his Calvinism and is seen through his understanding of Christian Hedonism. Christian Hedonism, an outgrowth of Piper's understanding of God's glory, may be the glue that binds his thoughts and allows him to see God as having more than one way of willing. As one grows in Christ, one glorifies God. When one desires to glorify God, he will share Christ with others, even if that means going to the remotest parts of the earth.

Finally, I demonstrated that Piper is internally consistent. What he stated in the beginning of his ministry is remarkably like what he stated at the end of his retirement from the pastorate. Piper would agree that as his understanding of God's glory as deepened, his understanding of the importance of living to the glory of God's name has increased, which in turn has deepened his passion to spread the gospel to the nations.

QUESTIONS FOR FURTHER STUDY

There are certain questions I did not attempt to answer. I did not look at the "correctness" of Calvinism or the issues in the human responsibility/sovereignty of God debate. Piper recognizes the tension and has an opinion, but he does not see the solution as either/or. In response to J. I. Packer calling the answer to the

---

4   For example, see: Thomas K. Ascol, "Calvinism, Evangelism and Founders Ministries," *The Founders Journal* 45 (Summer 2001): 1–21.

5   John Piper, *You Will Be Eaten by Cannibals! Courage in the Cause of World Missions. Lessons in the Life of John G. Paton.* Audio cd. Minneapolis: Desiring God Ministries, 2000.

question an "antinomy," an "appearance of contradiction between conclusions which seem equally logical, reasonable or necessary;" he states:

> [E]verything God does toward men—his commanding, his calling, his warning, his promising, his weeping over Jerusalem—everything is his means of creating situations which function as motives to elicit the acts of will which he has ordained to come to pass. In this way He ultimately determines all acts of volition (though not all in the same way) and yet holds man accountable only for those acts which they want most to do.[6]

I also did not examine whether Piper's thought is correct. Rather, I sought to determine if Piper was consistent. My purpose was to show that Piper's understanding of the glory of God via Calvinism – seen through the Two Wills of God Thesis – motivated his missiology. Examining the truth of Piper's argument would require detailed exegesis of the passages on the glory of God, a critique of other parts of his theology, and an appraisal of his missiology. Addressing these issues would require long, separate treatises.

---

6   John Piper, "A Response to J. I. Packer," <http://www.desiringgod.org/library/topics/doctrines_grace/packer.html>, site editor, Desiring God Ministries, March 1976, accessed on 5 February 2005.

SELECT BIBLIOGRAPHY

Aquinas, Thomas. *Summa Theologica*. Edited by English Dominican Fathers. Vol. 1 . New York: Beziger, 1947.

Ascol, Thomas K. "Calvinism, Evangelism and Founders Ministries." In *The Founders Journal* 45 (Summer 2001): 1–21.

Arminius, James. *The Works of Arminius*. Translated by James Nichols and William Nichols. Vol. 2. Grand Rapids: Baker, 1986. Reprint.

Augustine. *Enchiridion* 26:1 00. Quoted in John Calvin, *Institutes of the Christian Religion*. Edited by John T. McNeill. Translated by Ford Lewis Battles, 325. Vol. 2. Philadelphia: Westminster, 1960.

Basinger, David, and Randall Basinger, eds. *Predestination and Free Will: Four Views of Divine Sovereignty and Human Freedom*. Downers Grove, IL: InterVarsity, 1986.

Basinger, Randall G. "Exhaustive Divine Sovereignty." In *A Case for Arminianism*. Edited by Clark Pinnock. Grand Rapids: Zondervan, 1989.

Barrett, David. "Annual Statistical Table on Global Mission: 2002." *International Bulletin of Missionary Research* 26, no. 1 (January 2002): 22–23.

Barrett, David, George T. Kuruan, and Todd M. Johnson. *World Christian Encyclopedia: A Comparative Study of Churches and Religions—AD 30 to 2000*. Vol. 1 . Oxford: Oxford University Press, 2001.

Berkhof, Louis. *Systematic Theology*, 4th revised and enlarged ed. Grand Rapids: Eerdmans, 1994.

"Biography of John Piper." In *Desiring God Ministries*. <http://www. desiringgod.org/who_is_dgm/about_piper/piper_bio. html>. Accessed on 10 April 2003.

Boettner, Loraine. *Doctrine of Reformed Predestination*, 8th ed. Grand Rapids: Eerdmans, 1954.

Bonhoeffer, Dietrich. *The Cost of Discipleship*. London: SCM, 1976.

_____. *The Cost of Discipleship*. New York: Macmillan, 1963.

Bonk, Jonathan J. *Missions and Money. Affluence as a Western Missionary Problem*. Maryknoll, NY: Orbis, 1991.

Bosch, David. "Evangelism: A Holistic Approach." *Journal of Theology for Southern Africa* 36 (Sept 1 981): 46 53.

_____. "Evangelism: Theological Currents and Cross-currents Today." *International Bulletin of Missionary Research* 11 , no. 3 (July 1 987): 98–103.

_____. "In Search of a New Evangelical Understanding." *In Word and Deed: Evangelism and Social Responsibility*, ed. Bruce Nicholls, 63–83. Grand Rapids: Eerdmans, 1985.

_____. "Mission—An Attempt at a Definition." *Church Sense* (April 25, 1986): 11 .

_____. "Mission in Jesus' Way: A Perspective from Luke's Gospel." *Missionalia* 17 (April 1989): 3–21 .

_____. "Reflections on Biblical Models of Mission." In *Toward the 21ˢᵗ Century in Christian Mission*, ed. James M. Phillips and Robert T. Coote, 1 75–92. Grand Rapids: Eerdmans, 1993.

_____. "The Church in Dialogue: From Self-delusion to Vulnerability." *Missiology* 16 (April 1988): 131–47.

_____. "The Church Without Privileges." *Asfacts* 19 (September): 1977. Quoted in J. Kevin Livingston, "A Missiology of the Road: The Theology of Mission and Evangelism in the

Writings of David J. Bosch," 28–29. Ph.D. diss., University of Aberdeen, 1989.

_____. "The Question of Mission Today." *Journal of Theology for South Africa 1* (December 1972): 5–15.

_____. "The Structure of Mission: An Exposition of Matthew 28:1 6–20." In *Exploring Church Growth*, ed. Wilbert R. Shenk, 21 8–48. Grand Rapids: Eerdmans, 1983.

_____. "The Vulnerability of Mission." *Zeitschrift für Missionswissenschaft und Religionswissenschaft* 76, no. 3 (Jan 1 992): 201–16.

_____. *Theology of Religions*. Pretoria, South Africa: University of South Africa, 1977.

_____. *Transforming Mission: Paradigm Shifts in the Theology of Mission*. Maryknoll, NY: Orbis, 1 991 .

_____. "Vision for Mission." *International Review of Mission* 76, no. 301 (January 1 987): 8–15.

_____. *Witness to the World: The Christian Mission in Theological Perspective*. Atlanta: John Knox, 1980.

Boice, James Montgomery, and Philip Graham Ryken. *The Doctrines of Grace*. Wheaton, IL: Crossway, 2002.

Calvin, John. *Secret Providence*. Translated by James Lillie. 1840. Reprint, Albany, OR: Ages Software, 1998. CD ROM.

_____. *Institutes for Christian Religion*. Vols. 1–2. Edited by John T. McNeill. Translated by Ford Lewis Battles. Philadelphia: Westminster, 1960.

Carpenter, John B. "New England Puritans: Grandparents of Modern Protestant Missions," *Missiology: An International Review* XXX, no. 4 (Oct 2002), 519.

Clipsham, E. F. "Andrew Fuller and Fullerism: A Study in Evangelical Calvinism." *Baptist Quarterly* 20 (July 1963): 99–114.

Charnock, Steven. *The Existence and Attributes of God*. Vol. 2. Grand Rapids: Baker, 2000.

Commission on World Mission and Evangelism. "San Antonio: Report, Section One." *International Review of Mission* 78, nos. 31 1–1 2 (1989): 345–56.

Dabney, Robert L., and Jonathan Dickinson. *The Five Points of Calvinism*. Harrisonburg, VA: Sprinkle, 1992.

Daniel, Curt D. "Hyper-Calvinism and John Gill." Ph.D. diss., University of Edinburgh, 1983.

DeJong, J.A. *As the Waters Cover the Sea: Millennial Expectations in the Rise of Anglo-American Missions, 1640-1810*. Kampen, the Netherlands: J.H. Kok N.V., 1970.

Du Preez, J. "David Bosch's Theology of Religions: An Exercise in Humility." In *Mission in Creative Tension: A Dialogue with David Bosch*, ed. JNJ Krizinger and WA Saayman, 196. Pretoria, South Africa: South African Missiological Society, 1990.

Edwards, David L., and John Stott. *Evangelical Essentials: A Liberal–Evangelical Dialogue*. Downers Grove, IL: InterVarsity, 1988.

Edwards, Jonathan. "An Essay on the Trinity." In *Treatise on Grace and Other Posthumously Published Writings*, ed. Paul Helm, 99–131. Cambridge: James Clark, 1971.

_____. *Charity and Its Fruits*. Edinburgh: Banner of Truth, 1852. Reprint, 1969.

_____. "Concerning the Decrees in General, and Election in Particular." In *The Works of Jonathan Edwards*, Vol. 2, 516. Edinburgh: Banner of Truth, 1974.

_____. *Freedom of the Will*. Edited by Paul Ramsey. New Haven: Yale University Press, 1957.

_____. Miscellanies, #448. In *The Philosophy of Jonathan Edwards from this Private Notebooks*, ed. Harvey G. Townsend, 1 33. Westport, CT: Greenwood Press, 1955. Reprint, 1972.

_____. The End for Which God Created the World. Quoted in John Piper, *God's Passion for His Glory: Living the Vision of Jonathan Edwards*, 121–251. Wheaton, IL: Crossway, 1998.

_____. *The Works of President Edwards*. Edited by Edward Williams and Edward Parsons, Vols. 1–3. New York: Leavitt & Allen, 1855.

Erasmus, Desiderius. "On the Freedom of the Will." In *Luther and Erasmus: Free Will and Salvation*, ed. John Baillie, John T. McMeill, and Henry P. van Dusen, 35–97. Library of Christian Classics, Vol. 17. Philadelphia: Westminster, 1959.

Erickson, Millard. *Christian Theology*, 2d ed. Grand Rapids: Baker, 1998.

_____. "Hope for Those Who Haven't Heard? Yes, But ...." *Evangelical Missions Quarterly* 11 , no. 2 (April 1975): 1 24–25. Quoted in John Piper, *Let the Nations Be Glad!*, 2d ed. 1 14 n 7. Grand Rapids: Baker, 2003.

_____. *How Shall They Be Saved? The Destiny of Those Who Do Not Hear of Jesus*. Grand Rapids: Baker, 1996.

Feinberg, John. *No One Like Him: The Doctrine of God*. Wheaton, IL: Crossway, 2001.

Finney, Charles. *Finney's Systematic Theology*, new expanded ed. Complied and edited by Dennis Carroll, Bill Nicely, and L. G. Parkhurst. Minneapolis: Bethany, 1994.

Flanagan, Neal. "The What and How of Salvation in Luke-Acts." In *Sin, Salvation and the Spirit*, ed. D. Durken, 211. Collegeville: Liturgical, 1979. Quoted in David Bosch, "Mission in Jesus' Way," 11. *Missionalia* 17 (April 1989): 3–21.

Forster, R. T., and V. P. Marston. *God's Strategy in Human Strategy*. Wheaton, IL: Tyndale House, 1973.

Founders Ministries. "Index." In "Founders Ministries." http://www.founders.org/journal/index.html. Accessed on 29 January 2010.

Frame, John. *Apologetics for the Glory of God: An Introduction*. Phillipsburg, PA: Presbyterian & Reformed, 1994.

Fuller, Andrew. *Gospel Worthy of all Acceptation; or, The Duty of Sinners to Believe in Jesus Christ*. Boston: American Doctrinal Tract Society, 1846.

Fuller, Daniel. *Unity of the Bible: Unfolding God's Plan for Humanity*. Grand Rapids: Zondervan, 1991 .

Gates, Alan. "Perfection Growth." In *God, Man and Church Growth*, ed. A. R. Tippett, 1 28–42. Grand Rapids: Eerdmans, 1973.

Geisler, Norman. Chosen But Free: A Balanced View of Election. 2d ed. Minneapolis: Bethany: 2001.

_____.ed. "Evil, Problem Of." In *Baker Encyclopedia of Christian Apologetics*, 219. Grand Rapids: Baker, 1999.

Geisler, Norman, and Winfried Corduam. *Philosophy of Religion*, 2d ed. Grand Rapids: Baker, 1988.

George, Timothy. *Faithful Witness, The Life and Witness of William Carey*. Birmingham, AL: New Hope, 1991.

_____. "The Evangelical Revival and the Missionary Awakening." In *The Great Commission: Evangelicals and the History of World Missions*, ed. Martin Klauber and Scott Manetsch, 47. Nashville: Broadman & Holman, 2008.

_____. *Faithful Witness, the Life and Witness of William Carey*. Birmingham, AL: New Hope, 1991.

Gill, John. *A Complete Body of Doctrinal and Practical Divinity*. Reprint, Paris, AR: Baptist Standard Bearer, 1999. CD ROM.

_____. *Cause of God in Truth in Four Parts with a Vindication of Part 4*, new ed. London: W. H. Collinridge, 1855.

Gordon, Amy Glassner. "The First Protestant Missionary Effort: Why Did It Fail?" *International Bulletin for Missionary Research* 8, no 1 (Jan 1984), 12-14.

Grace Baptist Church. "International." In *Grace Baptist Church*. http://www.truegraceofgod.org/missions/international. Accessed on 29 January 2010.

Green, Jay. "Calvinism," 276. In *The Encyclopedia of Christianity*. Vol. 2. Marshallton, DE: National Foundation for Christian Education, 1968.

Grudem, Wayne. *Systematic Theology*. Grand Rapids: Zondervan, 1994.

Heppe, Heinrich. *Reformed Dogmatics*. Revised and expanded. Edited by Ernst Bizer. Translated by G. T. Thomson. London: George Allen and Unwin, 1860. Reprint, Grand Rapids: Baker, 1978.

Hick, John. "A Pluralist View." In *More than One Way: Four Views of Salvation in a Pluralistic World*, eds. Dennis Okholm and Timothy R. Phillips, 27–92. Grand Rapids: Zondervan, 1995.

_____. "The Non-Absoluteness of Christianity." In *The Myth of Christian Uniqueness: Towards a Pluralistic Theology of Religions*, eds. John Hick and Paul F. Knitter, 16–36. Maryknoll: Orbis, 1987.

_____."The Theological Challenge of Religious Pluralism." *In Christianity and Other Religions: Selected Readings*, rev and ed., John Hick and Brian Hebblewaite, 156–72. Oxford: Oneworld, 2001.

_____. "Whatever Path Men Choose is Mine." In *Christianity and Other Religions*, ed. John Hick and Brian Hebblethwaite, 188. Philadelphia: Fortress, 1980.

Hodge, Charles. *Systematic Theology*. Vol. 1 . Grand Rapids: Eerdmans. Reprint, Peabody, MA: Hendrickson, 2003.

Hopkins, Philip O. "Mission to Unreached People Groups." In *The Mission of God*, ed., Bruce Ashford. Nashville: Broadman and Holman, 2011.

Hughes, Philip E. "Grace." In *Evangelical Dictionary of Theology*, 2d ed., ed Walter A. Elwell, 519–22. Grand Rapids: Baker, 2001.

Kane, J. Herbert. *A Concise History of the Christian World: A Panoramic View of Missions from Pentecost to the Present*, revised ed. Grand Rapids: Baker, 1982.

Keller, Tim. "Advancing the Gospel into the 21 st Century. Part II: Gospel-Centered." In *Redeemer Presbyterian Church*. <http://www.redeemer2.com/resources/papers/missional.pdf>,site editor, Redeemer Presbyterian Church. Accessed on 3 February 2010.

_____. Advancing the Gospel into the 21 st Century. Part III: Context Sensitive." In *Redeemer Presbyterian Church*. http://www.redeemer2.com/themovement/issues/2004/feb/advancingthegospel_3.html. Accessed on 3 February 2010.

_____. "The Missional Church." In *Redeemer Presbyterian Church*. <http://www.redeemer2.com/resources/papers/missional.pdf>. Accessed on 3 February 2010.

Krizinger, J. J., and W. A. Saayman, eds. *Mission in Creative Tension: A Dialogue with David Bosch*. Pretoria, South Africa: South African Missiological Society, 1990.

Küng, Hans. *Eternal Life, Life After Death as a Medical, Philosophical, and Theological Problem*. New York: Doubleday, 1984.

Latourette, Kenneth S. *A History of the Expansion of Christianity: Three Centuries of Advance, A. D. 150—A. D. 1800*. Vol. 3, 25-26. New York: Cambridge University Press, 1939. In Donald Dan Smeeton, "William Tyndale's Suggestions for a Protestant Missiology." *Missiology: An International Review* 14, no 2 (April 1896), 174.

Lewis, C. S. *Reflections on the Psalms*. New York: Harcourt, Brace & World, 1958.

_____. *The Weight of Glory and Other Addresses*. Grand Rapids: Eerdmans, 1965.

Livingston, J. Kevin. "The Legacy of David J. Bosch," *International Bulletin of Missionary Research* 23, no. 1 (January 1999): 26–32.

_____. "A Missiology of the Road: The Theology of Mission and Evangelism in the Writings of David J. Bosch." Ph.D. diss., University of Aberdeen, 1 989.

Luther, Martin. *The Bondage of the Will*. Translated and edited by J. I. Packer and O. R. Johnston. Westwood, NJ: Revell, 1957.

_____. "On the Bondage of the Will." In John Baillie, *Luther and Erasmus: Free Will and Salvation*, eds. John T. McMeill, and Henry P. van Dusen, Library of Christian Classics. Vol. 1 7. Philadelphia: Westminster: 1954.

MacDonald, George. "Justice." In *George MacDonald: Creation in Christ*, ed. Rolland Hein, 63–81. Wheaton: Harold Shaw, 1976.

Marshall, I. Howard. "Universal Grace and Atonement in the Pastoral Epistles." In *The Grace of God and the Will of Man: A Case for Arminianism*, ed. Clark Pinnock, 56. Minneapolis: Bethany House, 1995.

McGavran, Donald. "Barred Populations and Missionaries." *International Review of Mission* 64 (Jan 1 975): 56–61 .

_____, ed. *Church Growth and Christian Mission*. New York: Harper & Row, 1965.

_____. "Contemporary Evangelical Theology of Mission." *In Contemporary Theologies of Mission*, eds. Arthur F. Glasser and Donald McGavran, 100–12. Grand Rapids: Baker, 1983.

_____, ed. *Critical Issues in Missions Tomorrow*. Chicago: Moody, 1972.

_____."Evangelism and Church Growth." *Church Growth Bulletin* 6 (July 1969): 87–88.

_____, ed. *Eye of the Storm: The Great Debate in Mission*. Waco: Word, 1972.

_____."My Pilgrimage in Mission." *International Bulletin of Missionary Research* 10, vol. 1 (January 1986): 53–54, 56–58.

_____."The Biblical Base from Which Adjustments are Made." In *Christopaganism or Indigenous Christianity*, eds. Tetsunao Yamamori and Charles R. Taber. 35–55. South Pasadena, CA: William Cary Library, 1975.

_____. *The Bridges of God: A Study in the Strategies of Missions*, revised ed. New York: Friendship, 1955.

_____. *The Clash Between Christianity and Cultures*. Washington: Canon, 1974.

_____. "The God Who Finds His Mission." *International Review of Mission* 51 (1962): 303–16.

_____. *Understanding Church Growth*, revised ed. Grand Rapids: Eerdmans, 1980.

McGavran, Donald, and Win Arn. *How to Grow a Church*. Glendale, CA: Regal, 1973.

_____. *Ten Steps for Church Growth*. New York: Harper & Row, 1977.

McGrath, Alister. *Iustitia Dei: A History of the Christian Doctrine of Justification*. Cambridge: Cambridge University Press, 1989. Reprint, 1997.

Mullins, E. Y. The *Christian Religion in Its Doctrinal Expression*. Nashville: Sunday School Board of the Southern Baptist Convention, 1917.

Murphy, Dale. *The Word of Truth: A Summary of Christian Doctrine Based on Biblical Revelation*. Grand Rapids: Eerdmans, 1981.

Murray, Iain. *The Forgotten Spurgeon*. Edinburgh: Banner of Truth, 1978.

Nettles, Thomas J. *By His Grace and For His Glory: A Historical, Theological, and Practical Study of the Doctrine of Grace in Baptist Life*. Grand Rapids: Baker, 1986.

_____. "Missions and Creeds (Part 2)." *The Founders Journal* 18 (Fall 1994): 13–14.

Netland, Harold. Dissonant Voices: *Religious Pluralism and the Question of Truth*. 1991. Reprint, Vancouver: Regent Publishers, 1998.

_____. *Encountering Religious Pluralism: The Challenge to Christian Faith and Mission*. Downers Grove, IL: InterVarsity, 2001.

Oden, Thomas C. *The Living God: Systematic Theology: Volume One*. Peabody, MA: Prince, 2001.

_____. *The Word of Life: Systematic Theology: Volume Two*. Peabody, MA: Prince, 1989.

Omanson, Roger L. "The Justification of God." *Review and Expositor* 82 (Spring 1 985): 283–84.

Osterhaven, M. E. "Will of God." In *Evangelical Dictionary of Theology*, 2d ed. Walter A. Elwell, ed., 1 276–78. Grand Rapids: Baker, 2001.

Padwick, Constance E. *Henry Martyn: Confessor of the Faith*. London: InterVarsity, 1953.

Palmer, Edwin. *The Five Points of Calvinism*. Grand Rapids: Baker, 1980.

Pascal, Blaise. *Pascal's Pensees*. Translated by W. F. Trotter. New York: E. P. Dutton, 1958.

Paton, John G. John G. Paton, D.D. Missionary to the New Hebrides: An Autobiography. London: Hodder & Stoughton, 1891.

Pinnock, Clark. *A Wideness of God's Mercy: The Finality of Jesus Christ in a World of Religions*. Grand Rapids: Zondervan, 1992.

_____. "Acts 4:1 2—No Other Name Under Heaven." In *Through No Fault of Their Own*, eds. William Crockett and James G. Sigountos, 113. Grand Rapids: Baker, 1991. Quoted in John Piper, *Let the Nations Be Glad! The Supremacy of God in Missions*, 2d ed., 1 25 n 23. Grand Rapids: Baker, 2003.

_____. "An Inclusivist View." In *More Than One Way: Four Views of Salvation in a Pluralistic World*, eds. Dennis Okholm and Timothy R. Phillips, 93–140. Grand Rapids: Zondervan, 1995.

_____. *Grace Unlimited*. Minneapolis: Bethany Fellowship, 1975.

_____, ed. *The Grace of God and the Will of Man: A Case for Arminianism*. Minneapolis: Bethany House, 1995.

_____. "The Conditional View." In Four Views of Hell. William Crockett, ed., 135–66. Grand Rapids: Zondervan, 1992.

_____. "The Destruction of the Finally Impenitent." Criswell Theological Review 4, no. 2 (Spring 1990): 243–59.

Piper, John and Wayne Grudem. *Recovering Biblical Manhood and Womanhood: A Response to Evangelical Feminism*. Wheaton, IL: Crossway, 1991.

Piper, John. "A Baptist Catechism: (Adapted By John Piper)." In *"Desiring God Ministries."* <http://www.desiringgod.org/library/what_we_believe/catechism.html>. Accessed 21 December 2004.

_____. *A Godward Life: 120 Daily Reading*. Sisters, OR: Multnomah, 1997.

_____. *A Godward Life, Book Two: Savoring the Sustenance of God in All of Life*. Sisters, OR: Multnomah, 1999.

_____. "A Mind in Love with God: The Private Life of a Modern Evangelical." In *"Desiring God Ministries."* <http://desiringgod.org/library/topics/edwards/edwards_mind.html>. Accessed 15 May 2003.

_____. "A Pastor's Role in World Missions ." In *"Desiring God Ministries."* <http://www.desiringgod.org/library/topics/pastors_role.html>. Accessed 3 March 2004.

_____. "A Response to J. I. Packer." In "*Desiring God Ministries.*" <http://www.desiringgod.org/library/topics/doctrines_grace/packer.html>. Accessed 5 February 2005.

_____. "A Response to Richard Mouw's Treatment of Christian Hedonism in The God Who Commands." In "*Desiring God Ministries.*" <http//www.desiringgod.org/library/topics/christian_hedonism/mouw.html>. Accessed 8 January 2004.

_____. "A Summary Theology of Prayer." In "*Desiring God Ministries.*" <http://desiringgod.org/library/fresh_words/2002/062602.html>. Accessed 1 6 January 2004.

_____. "A Vision of Biblical Complementarity Manhood and Womanhood Defined According to the Bible." In *Recovering Biblical Manhood and Womanhood: A Response to Evangelical Feminism*, eds. John Piper and Wayne Grudem, 43. Wheaton, IL: Crossway, 1991.

_____. "Adam, Christ, and Justification: Part Two." In "*Desiring God Ministries.*" <http://www.desiringgod.org/library/sermons/00/062500.html>. Accessed 22 April 2004.

_____. "Adam, Where Are You?" In "*Desiring God Ministries.*" <http://desiringgod. org/library/sermons/84/061784.html>. Accessed 22 January 2004.

_____. "Affirmation of Faith." In "*Desiring God Ministries.*" <http://www.desiringgod.org/library/what_we_believe/tbi_affirmation. html>. Accessed 6 June 2003.

_____. "All Things are From God, Through God, and To God. The Glory is All His." In "*Desiring God Ministries.*" <http://www.desiringgod.org/library/sermons/04/032804.html>. Accessed 21 December 2004.

_____. "An Open Letter to Rabbi Marcia Zimmerman." In *"Desiring God Ministries."* <http://www.desiringgod.org/library/fresh_words/2004/030304.html>. Accessed 29 November 2004.

_____. "Arming Yourself with the Purpose to Suffer." In *"Desiring God Ministries."* <http://www.desiringgod.org/library/sermons/94/1 00294.html>. Accessed 26 January 2004.

_____. "Beautifying the Body of Christ." In *"Desiring God Ministries."* <http://www.desiringgod.org/library/sermons/92/101192.html>. Accessed 2 December 2004.

_____. "Behold the Kindness and the Severity of God: The Echo and Insufficiency of Hell Part One." In *"Desiring God Ministries."* <http://www.desiringgod.org/library/sermons/92/061492/html>. Accessed 1 April 2004.

_____. "Biblical Texts to Show God's Zeal for His Own Glory." In *"Desiring God Ministries."* <http://www.desiringgod.org/ResourceLibrary/Articles/ByDate/2007/2510_Biblical_Texts_to_Show_Gods_Zeal_for_His_Own_Glory/>. Accessed on 5 February 2010.

_____. "Blessed Are the Persecuted." In *"Desiring God Ministries."* <http://www.desiringgod.org/library/sermons/86/031686.html>. Accessed 2 June 2004.

_____. "Boasting in Man is Doubly Excluded." In *"Desiring God Ministries."* <http://www.desiringgod.org/library/fresh_words/2003/030503.html>. Accessed 21 December 2004.

_____. "Books that Have Influenced Me the Most." In *"Desiring God Ministries."* <http://www.desiringgod.org/library/topics/leadership/books.html>. Accessed 6 August 2003.

_____. "Brothers, God is Love!" In *"Desiring God Ministries."* <http://www.desiringgod.org/library/topics/leadership/brothers_godislove.html>. Accessed 13 March 2003.

_____. "Called According to His Purpose." In "*Desiring God Ministries*." <http://www.desiringgod.org/library/sermons/85/101385.html>. Accessed 8 September 2003.

_____. "Called to Rejoice in Suffering: For an Eternal Weight of Glory." In "*Desiring God Ministries*." <http://desiringgod.org/library/sermons/92/090692.html>. Accessed 26 January 2004.

_____. "Called to Rejoice in Suffering: For Holiness and Hope." In "*Desiring God Ministries*." <http://desiringgod.org /library/sermons/92/081 692.html>. Accessed 23 January 2004.

_____. "Called to Rejoice in Suffering: That We Might Gain Christ." In "*Desiring God Ministries*." <http://desiringgod.org/library/sermons/92/082392.html>. Accessed 26 January 2004.

_____. "Called to Rejoice in Suffering: To Finish the Aim of Christ's Afflictions." In "*Desiring God Ministries*." <http://desiringgod.org/library/sermons/92/083092.html>. Accessed 26 January 2004.

_____. "Calling All Clay Pots: A Celebration of Ministry." In "*Desiring God Ministries*." <http://www.desiringgod.org/library/sermons/82/091282.html>. Accessed 2 June 2004.

_____. "Can Christians Be Held Hostage By the Sins of the Beloved." In "*Desiring God Ministries*." <http://www.desiringgod.org/library/fresh_words/1 999/030999.html>. Accessed 20 November 2004.

_____. "Can Joy Increase Forever?" In "*Desiring God Ministries*." <http://desiringgod.org/library/fresh_words/1 998/050598.html>. Accessed 15 May 2003.

_____. "Carnal Cash into Kingdom Currency." In "*Desiring God Ministries*." <http://www.desiringgod.org/library/topics/money/carnal_cash.html >. Accessed 20 January 2004.

_____. "Children, Heirs, Fellow Sufferers." In *"Desiring God Ministries."* <http://www.desiringgod.org/library/ sermons/02/042102.html>. Accessed 1 June 2004.

_____. "Christian Courage." In *"Desiring God Ministries."* <http://www.desiringgod.org/library/fresh_words/1 999/051199. html>. Accessed 2 June 2004.

_____. "Christ, Culture and Abortion." In "Desiring God Ministries." <http://www.desiringgod.org/library/sermons/00/1 22300.html>. Accessed 29 November 2004.

_____. "Christ: The Lion and the Lamb." In *"Desiring God Ministries."* <http://www.desiringgod.org/library/ sermons/86/032386.html>. Accessed 3 February 2005.

_____. "Christ's Power Is Made Perfect in Weakness." In *"Desiring God Ministries."* <http://www.desiringgod.org/library/ sermons/91/071491.html>. Accessed 3 June 2004.

_____. "Christ's Purposes in Evangelism." In *"Desiring God Ministries."* <http://www.desiringgod.org/library/ sermons/88/052288.html>. Accessed 3 June 2004.

_____. "Closed Countries and Retirement." In "Desiring God Ministries." <http://www.desiringgod.org/library/topics/missions/ retirement.html>. Accessed on 2 June 2004.

_____. "Conversion to Christ." In *"Desiring God Ministries."* <http://www. desiringgod.org/library/sermons/83/091883. html>. Accessed 10 February 2004.

_____. "Conversion: The Creation of a Christian Hedonist." In *"Desiring God Ministries."* <http://www.desiringgod.org/dg/ id36_m.htm>. Accessed 31 March 2004.

_____. *Counted Righteous in Christ: Should We Abandon the Imputation of Christ's Righteousness?* Wheaton, IL: Crossway, 2002.

_____. "Creation, Fall, Redemption and the Holy Spirit." In *"Desiring God Ministries."* <http://www.desiringgod.org/library/sermons/84/021284.html>. Accessed 5 September 2003.

_____. *Desiring God: Meditations of a Christian Hedonist,* 3d ed. Sisters, OR: Multnomah, 2003.

_____. "Displays of God Remove the Excuse for Failed Worship." In *"Desiring God Ministries."* <http://www.desiringgod.org/library/sermons/98/092798.html>. Accessed 10 January 2005.

_____. "Doing Mercy to Brothers of Jesus and the Broken Hearted." In *"Desiring God Ministries."* <http://www.desiringgod.org/library/sermons/04/1 00304.html>. Accessed 29 November 2004.

_____. "Doing Mercy to the Brothers of Jesus and the Broken Neighbor." In *"Desiring God Ministries."* <http://www.desiringgod.org/library/sermons/04/100304.html>. Accessed 21 November 2004.

_____. "Don't Be Anxious, Lay Up Treasures in Heaven." In *"Desiring God Ministries."* <http://desiringgod.org/library/sermons/03/ 030203.html>. Accessed 20 January 2004.

_____. *Don't Waste Your Life.* Wheaton, IL: Crossway, 2003.

_____. "Do Not Harden Your Heart in the Day of Trial." In *"Desiring God Ministries."* <http://www.desiringgod.org/library/sermons/96/081196.html>. Accessed 2 December 2004.

_____. "Do Not say 'I am Only a Youth.'" In *"Desiring God Ministries."* <http://www.desiringgod.org/library/sermons/89/090389.html>. Accessed 21 December 2004.

_____. "Driving Commands Behind World Missions at Bethlehem." In "*Desiring God Ministries.*" <http://www. desiringgod.org/library/sermons/99/110296.html>. Accessed 4 March 2004.

_____. "Enjoying God and the Transformation of Culture." In "*Desiring God Ministries.*" <http://desiringgod.org/library/ topics/edwards/edwards_enjoying_god. html>. Accessed 15 May 2003.

_____. "Eternal Security Is a Community Project." In "*Desiring God Ministries.*" <http://www.desiringgod.org/library/sermons/96/081 896.html>. Accessed 23 October 2003.

_____. "Everlasting Truth for the Joy of All Peoples." In "*Desiring God Ministries.*" <http://www.desiringgod.org/library/ sermons/03/102603.html>. Accessed 14 May 2004.

_____. "Every Race to Reign and Worship." In "*Desiring God Ministries.*" <http://www.desiringgod.org/library/ sermons/98/0111898>. Accessed 23 April 2004.

_____. "Execution, Escape, and Eaten By Worms: How the Word of God Grew." In "*Desiring God Ministries.*" <http:// www.desiringgod.org/librart/sermons/91/120191.html>. Accessed 2 June 2004.

_____. "Exodus for All the Earth." In "*Desiring God Ministries.*" <http://desiringgod.org/library/sermons/81/110881 .html>. Accessed 22 December 2003.

_____. "Fathers Who Give Hope." In "*Desiring God Ministries.*" <http://www. desiringgod.org/library/sermons/86/061 586. html>. Accessed 1 June 2004.

_____. *Filling up the Afflictions of Christ: The Cost of Bringing the Gospel to the Nations in the Lives of William Tyndale, Adoniram Judson, and John Paton.* Wheaton, IL: Crossway, 2009.

_____. "For God's Sake, Let Grace Be Grace." In "*Desiring God Ministries.*" <http://www.desiringgod.org/library/sermons/03/111603.html>. Accessed 21 December 2004.

_____. "For Whom Did Jesus Taste Death?" In "*Desiring God Ministries.*" <http://www.desiringgod.org/library/sermons/96/052696.html>. Accessed 8 September 2003.

_____. "Fulfilling the Law of Love: Education for Exaltation: Through the Spirit by Faith." In "*Desiring God Ministries.*" <http://www.desiringgod.org/library/sermons/00/022700.html>. Accessed 3 February 2004.

_____. "Go and Make Disciples, Baptizing Them." In "*Desiring God Ministries.*" <http://www.desiringgod.org/library/sermons/82/111482.html>. Accessed 22 November 2004.

_____. "God Can Turn This Around." In "*Desiring God Ministries.*" <http://desiringgod.org/library/fresh_words/2001/062501 .html>. Accessed 20 January 2004.

_____. "God Created Us for His Glory." In "*Desiring God Ministries.*" <http://www.desiringgod.org/library/sermons/80/072780.html>. Accessed 3 February 2005.

_____. "God Credits Faith as Righteousness." In "*Desiring God Ministries.*" <http://www.desiringgod.org/library/sermons/99/080199.html>. Accessed 29 March 2004.

_____. "God Did Not Spare His Own Son." In "*Desiring God Ministries.*" <http://www.desiringgod.org/sermons/02/081 802.html>. Accessed 29 March 2004.

_____. "God Has Given Us Good Hope Through Grace." In "*Desiring God Ministries.*" <http://www.desiringgod.org/library/sermons/87/090687.html>. Accessed 2 December 2004.

_____. "God is a Very Important Person." In "*Desiring God Ministries.*" <http://www.desiringgod.org/library/topics/gods_passion/god_very_important.html>. Accessed 8 March 2004.

_____. "God Works for Those Who Wait for Him." In "*Desiring God Ministries.*" <http://www.desiringgod.org/library/sermons/82/090582.html>. Accessed 1 November 2004.

_____. "God's Great Mercy and Our New Birth." In "*Desiring God Ministries.*" <http://www.desiringgod.org/library/sermons/93/101093.html>. Accessed 8 September 2003.

_____. "God's Covenant with Noah." In "*Desiring God Ministries.*" <http://www.desiringgod.org/library/sermons/83/1 1 2786.html>. Accessed 9 November 2004.

_____. "God's Invincible Purpose Part Five: Foundations for Full Assurance: God Called Us into Life and Hope." In "*Desiring God Ministries.*" <http://www.desiringgod.org/library/sermons/92/040592.html>. Accessed 21 November 2004.

_____. "God's Invincible Purpose: Part One: Foundations for Full Assurance." In "*Desiring God Ministries.*" <http://www.desiringgod.org/library/sermons/92/030192.html>. Accessed 21 December 2004.

_____. *God's Passion for His Glory: Living the Vision of Jonathan Edwards.* Wheaton, IL: Crossway, 1998.

_____. "God's Pursuit of Racial Diversity At Infinite Cost." In "*Desiring God Ministries.*" <http://www.desiringgod.org/library/sermons/01/011401.html>. Accessed 23 April 2004.

_____. "God's Response to Hypocrisy: Kindness and Judgment." In "*Desiring God Ministries.*" <http://www.desiringgod.org/library/sermons/98/1 1 2298.html>. Accessed on 9 November 2004.

_____. "God's Word Stands: Christ Came to Confirm It." In "*Desiring God Ministries*." <http://www.desiringgod.org/library/ sermons/02/122202html>. Accessed 22 December 2004.

_____. "Going Hard After a Holy God." In "*Desiring God Ministries*." <http://www.desiringgod.org/library/sermons/92/082392.html>. Accessed 3 June 2004.

_____. "Good Deeds and the Glory of God." In "*Desiring God Ministries*." <http://www.desiringgod.org/library/sermons/87/021 587p.html>. Accessed 20 November 2004.

_____. "Hallowed Be Thy Name: In All the Earth." In "*Desiring God Ministries*." <http://www.desiringgod.org/library/ sermons/84/110484.html>. Accessed on 1 January 2005.

_____. "He Is Like a Refiner's Fire." In "*Desiring God Ministries*." <http://www.desiringgod.org/library/sermons/87/1 1 2987. html>. Accessed on 2 September 2003.

_____. "He Commanded and They Were Created." In "*Desiring God Ministries*." <http://desiringgod.org/library/ sermons/81/100481 .html>. Accessed 4 December 2003.

_____. "He Saw the Grace of God and Was Glad." In "*Desiring God Ministries*." <http://www.desiringgof.org/library/ sermons/91/112491 .html>. Accessed 1 June 2004.

_____. "Heart's Desire." In "*Desiring God Ministries*." <http:// www.desiringgod.org/library/sermons/85/010685.html>. Accessed 24 February 2003.

_____. "Holy, Holy, Holy is the Lord of Hosts." In "*Desiring God Ministries.* " <http://www.desiringgod.org/library/ sermons/84/010184.html>. Accessed 31 December 2004.

_____. "Holy Faith, Worthy Gospel, World Vision: Andrew Fuller's Broadsides Against Sandemanianism, Hyper-Calvinism, and Global Unbelief." In *"Desiring God Ministries."* <http://www.desiringgod.org/ResourceLibrary/ConferenceMessages/ByConfeence/13/1977_Holy_Faith_Worthy_Gospel_World_Vision/>. Accessed on 5 February 2010.

_____. "Holy Women Who Hoped in God." In *"Desiring God Ministries."* <http://www.desiringgod.org/library/sermons/86/051186.html>. Accessed 17 June 2003.

_____. "How Does a Sovereign God Love?: A Reply to Thomas Talbot." In *"Desiring God Ministries."* <http://www.desiringgod.org/library/topics/doctrines_grace/sovereign_god_love.html>. Accessed 10 February 2005.

_____. "How Few There are Who Die So Hard: The Cost of Bringing Christ to Burma. Suffering and Success in the Life of Adoniram Judson." In *"Desiring God Ministries."* <http://www.desiringgod.org/library/biographies/03/judson.html>. Accessed 31 December 2004.

_____. "How Shall People Be Saved [Part One] ." In *"Desiring God Ministries."* <http://www.desiringgod.org/library/sermons/03/060103.html>. Accessed 13 April 2004.

_____. "How Shall People Be Saved: Part Two." In *"Desiring God Ministries."* <http://www.desiringgod.org/library/sermons/03/083103.html>. Accessed 22 January 2004.

_____. "How the Called Receive An Eternal Inheritance." In *"Desiring God Ministries."* <http://www.desiringgod.org/library/sermons/97/012697.html>. Accessed 21 December 2004.

_____. "How to Do Good So God Gets the Glory." In *"Desiring God Ministries."* <http://www.desiringgod.org/library/sermons/80/080380.html>. Accessed 20 November 2004.

_____. "How To Drink Orange Juice to the Glory of God." In *"Desiring God Ministries."* <http://www.desiringgod.org/library/ topics/sin/orange_juice.html>. Accessed 2 September 2003.

_____. "I am God Almighty, Be Fruitful and Multiply: I Have Other Sheep." In *"Desiring God Ministries."* <http://www. desiringgod.org/library/sermons/96/030396.html>.Accessed 4 December 2004.

_____. "I Have Other Sheep That Are Not of This Fold." In *"Desiring God Ministries."* <http://www.desiringgod.org/library/ sermons/85/111085/.html>. Accessed 26 May 2004.

_____. "I Will Be Gracious To Whom I Will Be Gracious." In *"Desiring God Ministries."* <http://www.desiringgod.org/ library/sermons/84/092384.html>. Accessed 1 2 January 2005.

_____. "I Will Build My Church—From All Peoples." In *"Desiring God Ministries."* <http://www.desiringgod.org/library/ sermons/01/102801.html>. Accessed 29 November 2004.

_____. "I Will Raise Up for David a Righteous Branch." In *"Desiring God Ministries."* <http://www.desiringgod.org/library/ sermons/81/121381.html>. Accessed 23 December 2003.

_____. "I Will Sing Praises to You Among the Nations." In *"Desiring God Ministries."* <http://www.desiringgod.org/library/ sermons/91/062391 .html>. Accessed 19 May 2004.

_____. In Retirement of William Piper, 120 min, Special Collections. *Rogma* 1998. VHS, videocassette.

_____. "Invitation from John Piper." In *"Desiring God Ministries."* <http://www.desiringgod.org/news_ events/edwards/invitation.html>. Accessed 19 June 2003.

_____. "Is God for Us or for Himself." In "*Desiring God Ministries.*" <http://www.desiringgod.org/library/sermons/80/081 080. html>. Accessed 9 December 2004.

_____. "Is God Less Glorious Because He Ordained that Evil Be? Jonathan Edwards on the Decrees of God." In "*Desiring God Ministries.*" <http://desiringgod.org/library/topics/suffering/god_and_evil.html>. Accessed 15 May 2003.

_____. "Is the Glory of God at Stake in God's Foreknowledge of Human Choices? Jonathan Edwards' Response to Gregory Boyd." In "*Desiring God Ministries.*" <http://desiringgod.org/library/topics/foreknowledge/glory_foreknowledge. html>. Accessed 1 5 May 2003.

_____. "Is There Good Anxiety." In "*Desiring God Ministries.*"<http://www.desiringgod.org/library/sermons/81/042181.html>. Accessed 14 December 2004.

_____. "Jesus Christ: Alive and with Us to the End." In "*Desiring God Ministries.*" <http://www.desiringgod.org/library/sermons/00/041200.html>. Accessed 01 November 2004.

_____. "Jesus is the Christ the Son of God." In "*Desiring God Ministries.*" <http://www.desiringgod.org/library/sermons/91/100691.html>. Accessed 22 April 2004.

_____. "Jesus is the Christ the Son of God." In "*Desiring God Ministries.*" <http://www.desiringgod.org/librart/topics/christ/the_unparralleled_passion_of_jesus_christ.html>. Accessed 22 April 2004.

_____. "Jesus Is Precious as the Foundation of the Family." In" *Desiring God Ministries.*" <http://desiringgod.org/library/sermons/82/0321 82.html>. Accessed 22 January 2004.

_____. "Jesus is Precious Because He Gives Eternal Life." In "*Desiring God Ministries*." <http://www.desiringgof.org/library/ sermons/82/022882.html>. Accessed 26 September 2003.

_____. "Jesus is Precious Because He Removes Our Guilt." In "*Desiring God Ministries*." <http://www.desiringgod.org/ library/sermons/82/022182.html>. Accessed 22 April 2004.

_____. "Joy Purchased." In "*Desiring God Ministries*." <http:// www.desiringgod.org/library/sermons/89/020589.html>. Accessed 20 March 2003.

_____. "Joy Recovered." In "*Desiring God Ministries*." <http:// www.desiringgod.org/library/sermons/89/021289.html>. Accessed 21 November 2004.

_____. "Joy Through the Fiery Test of Faith." In "*Desiring God Ministries*." <http://desiringgod.org/library/sermons/93/102493. html>. Accessed 26 January 2004.

_____. "Let All the Peoples Praise Thee." In "*Desiring God Ministries*." <http://www.desiringgod. org/library/ sermons/86/110986.html>. Accessed 19 May 2004.

_____. "Let Marriage Be Held in Honor Among All." In "*Desiring God Ministries*." <http://www.desiringgod.org/library/ sermons/91/081191.html>. Accessed 1 0 February 2004.

_____. "Let the Nations Be Glad!" In "*Desiring God Ministries*." <http://www.desiringgod.org/library/sermons/93/1 1 0793. html>. Accessed 14 May 2003.

_____. *Let the Nations Be Glad! The Supremacy of God in Missions*, 2d ed. Grand Rapids: Baker, 2003.

_____. "Let Us Go with Jesus, Bearing Reproach." In "*Desiring God Ministries*." <http://www.desiringgod.org/library/ sermons/97/100283.html>. Accessed 1 June 2004.

_____. "Love." In "*Desiring God Ministries.*" <http://www. desiringgod.org/library/sermons/83/100283.html>. Accessed 2 March 2004.

_____. "Loving God for Who He Is: A Pastor's Perspective." In "*Desiring God Ministries.*" <http://www.desiringgod.org/topics/leadership/loving_god.html>. Accessed 29 November 2004.

_____. "Luther, Bunyan, Bible and Pain." In "*Desiring God Ministries.*" <http://www.desiringgod.org/library/fresh_words/1999/011999.html>. Accessed 2 June 2004.

_____. "Marriage." In "*Desiring God Ministries.*" <http://desiringgod.org/library/sermons/83/101683.html>. Accessed 20 January 2004.

_____. "Male and Female He Created Them in the Image of God." In "*Desiring God Ministries.*" <http://www.desiringgod.org/library/sermons/89/051489.html>. Accessed 2 September 2003.

_____. "Mercy to the Nations." In "*Desiring God Ministries.*" <http://www.desiringgod.org/library/sermons/89/110589.html>. Accessed 3 February 2004.

_____. "Missions and the End of History." In "*Desiring God Ministries.*" <http://www.desiringgod. org/library/sermons/97/102697.html>. Accessed 1 March 2004.

_____. "Missions: The Battle Cry of Christian Hedonism." In "*Desiring God Ministries.*" <http://www.desiringgod.org/library/sermons/83/111383.html>. Accessed 30 December 2004.

_____. "Money." In "*Desiring God Ministries.*" <http://desiringgod.org/library/sermons/83/100983.html>. Accessed 20 January 2004.

_____. "Not Ashamed of the Gospel." In *"Desiring God Ministries."* <http://www.desiringgod.org/library/sermons/98/060498. html>. Accessed 29 November 2004.

_____. "Nothing Can Separate Us from the Love of Christ." In *"Desiring God Ministries."* <http://www.desiringgod.org/ library/sermons/02/090802.html>. Accessed 2 June 2004.

_____. "O Be Not Mere Shadows, Echoes, and Residue." In *"Desiring God Ministries."* <http://www.desiringgod.org/library/ fresh_words/1999/100599.html>. Accessed 20 November 2004.

_____. "O Lord, Open My Eyes!" In *"Desiring God Ministries."* <http://desiringgod.org/library/sermons/98/010498.html>. Accessed 14 January 2004.

_____. "O, That You Knew the Terms of Peace." In *"Desiring God Ministries."* <http://www.desiringgod.org/library/18/041281. html>. Accessed 20 November 2004.

_____. "Old and Young Shall Dream Together." In *"Desiring God Ministries."* <http://www.desiringgod.org/library/ sermons/89/091089.html>. Accessed 27 May 2004.

_____. "Overflowing Grace for All Who Believe: The Conversion of the Chief of Sinners." In *"Desiring God Ministries."* <http:// www.desiringgod.org/library/sermons/91/060991.html>. Accessed 8 September 2003.

_____. "Pastoral Thoughts on the Doctrine of Election." In *"Desiring God Ministries."* <http://www.desiringgod.org/library/ sermons/03/113003.html>. Accessed 21 December 2004.

_____. "Peculiar Doctrines, Public Morals, and the Political Welfare: Reflections on the Life and Labor of William Wilberforce." In *"Desiring God Ministries."* <http://desiringgod.org/library/ biographies/02wilberforce.html>. Accessed 20 November 2004.

_____. *Pierced by the Word*. Sisters, OR: Multnomah, 2003.

_____. "Perfect Love Casts of Fear." In *"Desiring God Ministries."* <http://www.desiringgod.org/library/sermons/85/052685.html>. Accessed 4 November 2004.

_____. "Perfect Love Casts of Fear." In *"Desiring God Ministries."* <http://www.desiringgod.org/library/sermons/85/052685.html>. Accessed 4 November 2004.

_____. "Prayer." In *"Desiring God Ministries."* <http://desiringgod.org/library/sermons/83/1 02383.html>. Accessed 10 February 2004.

_____. "Prayer: The Work of Missions." In *"Desiring God Ministries."* <http://desiringgod.org/library/topics/prayer/prayer_missions.html>. Accessed 16 January 2004.

_____. "Praying from the Fullness of the Word." In *"Desiring God Ministries."* <http://desiringgod.org/library/sermons/96/122996.html>. Accessed 19 January 2004.

_____. "Prolegomena to Understanding Romans 9:4–1 5: An Interpretation of Exodus 33:1 9." *Journal of the Evangelical Theological Society*, 22, no. 3 (September 1 979): 203–16.

_____. "Quest: Joy. Found: Christ." In *"Desiring God Ministries."* <http://www.desiringgod.org/library/sermons/03/042003.html>. Accessed 29 November 2004.

_____. "Quest for Joy: Six Biblical Truths." In *"Desiring God Ministries."* <http://www.desiringgod.org/library/what_we_believe/quest4joy.html>. Accessed 21 November 2004.

_____. "Raising Children Who Hope in the Triumph of God." In *"Desiring God Ministries."* <http://www.desiringgod.org/library/sermons/88/050888.html>. Accessed 17 June 2003.

_____. "Risk and the Cause of God." In *"Desiring God Ministries."* <http://www.desiringgod.org/library/sermons/87/050387.html>. Accessed 3 June 2004.

_____. "Ruth: Sweet and Bitter Providence." In *"Desiring God Ministries."* <http://desiringgod.org/library/sermons/84/070784.html>. Accessed 23 January 2004.

_____. "Sealed by the Spirit to the Day of Redemption." In *"Desiring God Ministries."* <http://www.desiringgod.org/library/sermons/84/050684.html>. Accessed 20 March 2003.

_____. *Seeing and Savoring Jesus Christ.* Wheaton, IL: Crossway, 2001.

_____. "Spreading Spiritual Power through Persecution." In *"Desiring God Ministries."* <http://www.desiringgod.org/library/sermons/91/050591.html>. Accessed 2 June 2004.

_____. "Strengthened to Suffer: Christ, Noah, and Baptism." In *"Desiring God Ministries."* <http://www.desiringgod.org/library/sermons/94/092594.html>. Accessed 21 November 2004.

_____. "Suffering for the Sake of the Body: The Pursuit of People Through Pain." In *"Desiring God Ministries."* <http://www.desiringgod.org/library/tbi/suffering.html>. Accessed on 2 June 2004.

_____. "Summary of the Sovereignty of God in Salvation: The 'Five Points' of Calvinism." In *"Desiring God Ministries."* <http://www.desiringgod.org/library/topics/doctrines_grace/summary.html>. Accessed 19 September 2003.

_____. "Surely He Has Borne Our Griefs." In *"Desiring God Ministries."* <http://www.desiringgod.org/library/sermons/93/031493.html>. Accessed 18 May 2004.

_____. "Sustained By the Faithfulness in God." In *"Desiring God Ministries."* <http://www.desiringgod.org/library/sermons/88/011788.html>. Accessed 29 October 2003.

_____. "Sustained By Sovereign Grace–Forever." In *"Desiring God Ministries."* <http://desiringgod.org/library/sermons/96/061696.html>. Accessed 26 January 2004.

_____. "Take Care How You Listen!" In *"Desiring God Ministries."* <http://www.desiringgod.org/library/sermons/98/022298.html>. Accessed 29 November 2004.

_____. "Take Heed How You Hear!" In *"Desiring God Ministries."* <http://desiringgod.org/library/fresh_words/1998/030198.html>. Accessed 16 January 2004.

_____. "Ten Effects of Believing in the Five Points of Calvinism." In *"Desiring God Ministries."* <http://www.desiringgod.org/library/topics/doctrine_grace/ten_effects.html>. Accessed 4 January 2005.

_____. "Thankful for the Love of God! Why?" In *"Desiring God Ministries."* <http://www.desiringgod.org/library/sermons/01/111801.html>. Accessed 17 June 2003.

_____. "Thanks Be to God for His Inexpressible Gift." In *"Desiring God Ministries."* <http://www.desiringgod.org/library/sermons/89/111989/html>. Accessed 21 November 2004.

_____. "That All the Nations Might Hear." In "Desiring God Ministries." <http://www.desiringgod.org/library/sermons/00/102900.html>. Accessed 27 May 2004.

_____. "The Absolute Sovereignty of God." In "*Desiring God Ministries.*" <http://desiringgod.org/library/sermons/02/110302.html>. Accessed 24 April 2003.

_____. "The Age of Ignorance is Over." In *Desiring God Ministries.*"<http://desiringgod.org/library/sermons/87/0621 87.html>. Accessed 9 April 2004.

_____. "The Argument of Romans 9:14–16." In "*Desiring God Ministries.*" <http:www.desiringgod.org/library/topics/doctrine_grace/romans_9.html>. Accessed 19 September 2003.

_____. "The Author of the Greatest Letter Ever Written." In "*Desiring God Ministries.*" <http://www.desiringgod.org/library/sermons/98/042698.html>. Accessed 8 May 2003.

_____. "The Bible." In "*Desiring God Ministries.*" <http://desiringgod.org/library/sermons/83/103083.html>. Accessed 15 January 2004.

_____. "The Cosmic Church." In "*Desiring God Ministries.*" <http://www.desiringgod.org/library/sermons/81/032281/html>.Accessed 9 April 2004.

_____. "The Demonstration of God's Righteousness and Mother's Day." In "*Desiring God Ministries.*" <http://www.desiringgod.org/library/sermons/99/050999.html>. Accessed 29 November 2004.

_____. "The Demonstration of God's Righteousness: Part Three." In "*Desiring God Ministries.*" <http://www.desiringgod.org/library/sermons/99/052399.html>. Accessed on 29 November 2004.

_____. "The Doctrine of Perseverance." In "*Desiring God Ministries.*" <http://www.desiringgod.org/library/topics/racial_harmony/sovereignty_soul_dynamic. html>. Accessed 9 February 2004.

_____. *"The Duty: Faith." In "Desiring God Ministries."* <http://desiringgod.org/library/sermons/94/121894.html>. Accessed 13 March 2003.

_____. "The Elect Are Kept By the Power of God." In *Desiring God Ministries."* <http://www.desiringgod.org/library/sermons/93/101793.html>. Accessed 23 October 2003.

_____. "The Emergence of Sin and Misery." In *"Desiring God Ministries."* <http://desiringgod.org/library/sermons/81/101181.html>. Accessed 22 December 2003.

_____. "The Evil Origin of a Good King." In *"Desiring God Ministries."* <http://www.desiringgod.org/library/sermons/81/120681.html>. Accessed 23 December 2003.

_____. "The Fame of His Name and the Freedom of Mercy." In *"Desiring God Ministries."* <http://desiringgod.org/library/sermons/03/020203.html>. Accessed 9 March 2003.

_____. "The Freedom and Justice of God in Unconditional Election." In *"Desiring God Ministries."* <http://desiringgod.org/library/sermons/03/011203.html>. Accessed 11 March 2003.

_____. "The Fruit of Hope: Boldness." In *"Desiring God Ministries."* <http://www.desiringgod.org/library/sermons/86/072086.html>. Accessed 31 December 2004.

_____. "The God-Centered Ground for Saving Grace: Grace Upon Grace: The Incomparable Riches of God." In *"Desiring God Ministries."* <http://www.desiringgod.org/library/topics/gods_passion/god_centered_ground html>. Accessed 21 December 2004.

_____. "The Greatest of These is Love: But I Say to You, Love Your Enemies Part One." In *"Desiring God Ministries."* <http://www.desiringgod.org/library/sermons/95/051495.html>. Accessed 08 November 2004.

_____. "The Greatest of These is Love: Love Your Neighbor As You Love Yourself Part One." In "*Desiring God Ministries.*" <http://wwwdesiringgod.org/library/sermons/95/043095. html>. Accessed 24 February 2003.

_____. "The Greatest of These is Love: Summer Is for Seeing and Showing Christ." In "*Desiring God Ministries.*" <http:// www.desiringgod.org/library/sermons/95/061195.html>. Accessed 16 July 2003.

_____. "The Greatest Thing in the World." In "*Desiring God Ministries.*" <http://www.desiringgod.org/library/ sermons/01/090201.html>. Accessed 9 December 2004.

_____. "The Happiness of God." In "*Desiring God Ministries.*" <http://www.desiringgod.org/library/sermons/83/091183. html>. Accessed 18 December 2003.

_____. *The Hidden Smile of God: The Fruit of Affliction in the Lives of John Bunyan, William Cowper, and David Brainerd.* Wheaton, IL: Crossway, 2001.

_____. "The Hour Has Come for the Son of Man to Be Glorified." In "*Desiring God Ministries.*" <http://www.desiringgod.org/ library/sermons/85/0331 85.html>. Accessed 4 January 2005.

_____. "The Inner Essence of Worship." In "*Desiring God Ministries.*" <http://desiringgod.org/library/sermons/97/111697. html>. Accessed 16 January 2004.

_____. *The Justification of God: An Exegetical and Theological Study of Romans 9:1–23*, 2d ed. Grand Rapids: Baker, 2001.

_____. "The Lord Is Great and Does Wondrous Things." In "*Desiring God Ministries.*" <http://www.desiringgod.org/library/ sermons/91/042891.html>. Accessed 18 May 2004.

_____. "The Lord Stood by Me." In *"Desiring God Ministries."*
<http://www.desiringgod.org/library/sermons/90/042290.
html>. Accessed 17 June 2003.

_____. "The Mission and Vision of Bethlehem Baptist Church
Volume 12: Radical Reconciliation Unpacking the Master
Planning Team Document Unfolding Fresh Initiative Three
Fresh Initiatives for the Immediate Future of Our Mission." In
"Desiring God Ministries." <http://www.desiringgod.org/library/
sermons/86/01 1496.html>. Accessed 2 September 2003.

_____. "The Missionary Challenge in Paul's Life." In *"Desiring
God Ministries."* <http://www.desiringgod.org/library/
sermons/85/110785.html>. Accessed 18 May 2004.

_____. "The Pastor as Theologian: Reflections on the Ministry
of Jonathan Edwards." In *"Desiring God Ministries."* <http://
desiringgod.org/library/biographies/88edwards.html>. Accessed
15 May 2003.

_____. "The Pleasure of God in Election." In *"Desiring
God Ministries."* <http://www.desiringgod.org/library/
sermons/87/022287.html>. Accessed 26 September 2003.

_____. "The Pleasure of God in His Creation." In *"Desiring
God Ministries."* <http://www.desiringgod.org/library/
sermons/87/020887.html>. Accessed 18 December 2003.

_____. "The Pleasure of God in His Name." In *"Desiring
God Ministries."* <http://www.desiringgod.org/library/
sermons/87/021587.html>. Accessed 1 December 2004.

_____. *The Pleasures of God: Meditations on God's Delight in Being
God*, rev. and expanded ed. Sisters, OR: Multnomah, 2000.

_____. "The Purpose and Perseverance of Faith." In *"Desiring
God Ministries."* <http://www.desiringgod.org/library/
sermons/99/101099.html>. Accessed 23 October 2003.

_____. "The Relationship Between Diversified Domestic Ministries and Frontier Missions." In "*Desiring God Ministries*." <http://www.desiringgod.org/library/sermons/84/111884.html>. Accessed 1 March 2004.

_____. "The Revelation of God's Righteousness Where There Is No Church." In "*Desiring God Ministries*." <http://www.desiringgod.org/library/sermons/99/110799.html>. Accessed 1 March 2004.

_____. *The Smile of God: The Fruit of Affliction in the Lives of John Bunyan, William Cowper, and David Brainerd*. Wheaton, IL: Crossway, 2001.

_____. "The Sovereignty of God and the Soul Dynamic." In "*Desiring God Ministries*." <http://www.desiringgod.org/library/topics/racial_harmony/sovereignty_soul_dynamic.html>. Accessed 9 February 2004.

_____. *The Supremacy of God in Preaching*. Grand Rapids: Baker, 1990.

_____. "The Swan is Not Silent." In "*Desiring God Ministries*." <http://www/desiringgod.org/library/biographies/98augustine.html>. Accessed 10 February 2004.

_____. "The Word of Faith We Proclaim: Part One." In "*Desiring God Ministries*." <http://www.desiringgod.org/library/sermons/03/051803.html>. Accessed 13 April 2004.

_____. "The Word of Faith We Proclaim: Part Two." In "*Desiring God Ministries*." <http://www.desiringgod.org/library/sermons/03/052503.html>. Accessed 13 April 2004.

_____. "The Wrath of God Against Ungodliness and Unrighteousness [Part 1] ." In "*Desiring God Ministries*." <http://www.desiringgod.org/library/sermons/98/083098.html>. Accessed 25 March 2004.

_____. "The Wrath of God Against Ungodliness and Unrighteousness [Part 2]." In "*Desiring God Ministries.*"<http://www.desiringgod.org/library/sermons/98/091 398.html>. Accessed 25 March 2004.

_____. "There is No Partiality with God [Part One]." In "*Desiring God Ministries.*" <http://www.desiringgod.org/library/sermons/98/122798.html>. Accessed 29 November 2004 .

_____. "There is No Partially with God [Part Two] ." In "*Desiring God Ministries.*" <http://www.desiringgod.org/library/sermons/99/013199.html>. Accessed 10 January 2005.

_____. "Thirty Stanzas." In "*Desiring God Ministries.*" <http://www.desiringgod.org/library/poems/98/thirty_stanzas.html>. Accessed 1 5 May 2003.

_____. "Those Whom He Foreknew He Predestined." In "*Desiring God Ministries.*" <http://www.desiringgod.org/library/sermons/85/101385.html>. Accessed 1 0 January 2005.

_____. "Those Whom He Predestined He Also Called: Part One." In "*Desiring God Ministries.*" <http://www.desiringgod.org/library/sermons/85/102085.html>. Accessed 9 February 2004.

_____. "Those Whom He Predestined He Also Called: Part Two." In "*Desiring God Ministries.*" <http://www.desiringgod.org/library/sermons/85/1 02085p.html>. Accessed 8 September 2003.

_____. "Thy Word I Have Treasured in My Heart." In "*Desiring God Ministries.*" <http://desiringgod.org/library/sermons/97/010597.html>. Accessed 15 January 2004.

_____. "To Him Be Glory Forevermore." In "*Desiring God Ministries.*" <http://www.desiringgod.org/ResourceLibrary/

Sermons/ByTopic/3/1 914_To_Him_Be_Glory_Forevermore/>. Accessed on 5 February 2010.

_____. "To Live Upon God that is Invisible: Suffering and Service in the Life of John Bunyan." In "*Desiring God Ministries.*" <http://www.desiringgod.org/library/biographies/99bunyan. html>. Accessed 1 June 2004.

_____. "Tolerance, Truth-telling, Violence, and Law: Principles for How Christians Should Relate to Those of Other Faiths: Spreading a Passion for the Supremacy of Jesus Christ in a Pluralistic and Hostile World Where National Identity and Religious Identity Are Blurred." In "*Desiring God Ministries.*" <http://www.desiringgod.org/library/topics/culture/tolerance_ principles.html>. Accessed 20 November 2004.

_____. "Toward the Tithe and Beyond." In "*Desiring God Ministries.*" <http://www.desiringgod.org/library/sermons/95/091095.html>. Accessed 10 February 2004.

_____. "Training the Next Generation of Evangelical Pastors and Missionaries." In "*Desiring God Ministries.*" <http://www. desiringgod.org/library/topics/leadership/train_next.html>. Accessed 5 March 2004.

_____. "Treating Delight as Duty is Controversial." In "*Desiring God Ministries.*" <http://www.desiringgod.org/library/fresh_ words/2001/102401 .html>. Accessed 29 November 2004.

_____. "Unconditional Election and the Invincible Purpose of God." In "*Desiring God Ministries.*"<http://www.desiringgof. org/library/sermons/02/1 21 502.html>. Accessed 29 October 2003.

_____. "Was Jonathan Edwards a Christian Hedonist?" In "*Desiring God Ministries.*" <http://desiringgod.org/library/ topics/christian_hedonism/edwards. html>. Accessed on 15 May 2003.

_____. "We Rejoice in Our Tribulations." In *"Desiring God Ministries."* <http://www.desiringgof.org/library/sermons/99/111499.html>. Accessed 01 June 2004.

_____. "What Answers Do Prayers Depend On?: Part2." In *"Desiring God Ministries."* <http://www.desiringgod.org/library/sermons/81/012581.html>. Accessed 21 November 2004.

_____. "What God Has Cleansed Do Not Call Common." In *"Desiring God Ministries."* <http://www.desiringgod.org/library/sermons/91/102091.html>. Accessed 12 April 2004.

_____. "What Is Baptism and Does it Save?" In *"Desiring God Ministries."* <http://www.desiringgod.org/library/sermons/97/051897.html>. Accessed 21 November 2004.

_____. "What Is the Will of God and How Do We Know It?" In *"Desiring God Ministries."* <http://www.desiringgod.org/library/sermons/04/082204.html>. Accessed 18 October 2004.

_____. "What Jesus Did After the Beginning." In *"Desiring God Ministries."* <http://www.desiringgod.org/library/sermons/90/091690.html>. Accessed 29 November 2004.

_____. "What the Law Could Not Do, God Did, Sending Christ." In *"Desiring God Ministries."* <http://www.desiringgod.org/library/sermons/01/101401.html>. Accessed 29 November 2004.

_____. "What We Believe About the Five Points of Calvinism." In *"Desiring God Ministries."* <http://desiringgod.org/library/topics/doctrines_grace/tulip.html>. Accessed 15 May 2000.

_____. "Whatever is not from Faith is Sin." In *"Desiring God Ministries."* <http://desiringgod.org/library/sermons/80/082480.html>. Accessed 1 8 November 2003.

_____. "Where is the Promise of His Appearing." In "*Desiring God Ministries*." <http://www.desiringgod.org/library/sermons/82/060682.html>. Accessed 4 January 2005.

_____. "Why I Did Not Say, 'God Did Not Cause the Calamity, but He Can Use it for Good.'" In "*Desiring God Ministries*." <http://www.desiringgod.org/library/fresh_words/2001/091701.html>. Accessed 3 December 2003.

_____. "Why Does It Matter Which Came First: Circumcision or Justification?" "*Desiring God Ministries*."<http://www.desiringgod.org/library/sermons/99/082299.html>. Accessed 18 May 2004.

_____. "Why Hope Grace!" In "*Desiring God Ministries*." <http://www.desiringgod.org/library/sermons/86/041386.html>. Accessed 21 December 2004.

_____. "Why the Law Was Given." In "*Desiring God Ministries*." <http://desiringgod.org/library/sermons/81/111581.html>. Accessed 22 December 2003.

_____. "Why We Can Rejoice in Suffering." In "*Desiring God Ministries.*"<http://desiringgod.org/library/sermons/94/102394.html>. Accessed 26 January 2004.

_____. "Worship God!" In "*Desiring God Ministries*." <http://desiringgod.org/library/sermons/91/091591.html>. Accessed 10 February 2004.

_____. "Worship is an End in Itself." In "*Desiring God Ministries.*" <http://desiringgod.org/library/sermons/81/091381.html>. Accessed 9 January 2004.

_____. "Worship the Risen Christ." In "*Desiring God Ministries*." <http://www.desiringgod.org/library/sermons/83/040383.html>. Accessed 22 November 2004.

_____. "You Have Filled Jerusalem with Your Teaching." In *"Desiring God Ministries."* <http://www.desiringgod.org/library/sermons/91/030391>. Accessed 4 January 2005.

_____. "You Shall Receive Power Till Jesus Comes." In *"Desiring God Ministries."* <http://www.desiringgod.org/library/sermons/90/093090.html>. Accessed 22 November 2004.

_____. *You Will Be Eaten by Cannibals! Courage in the Cause of World Missions. Lessons in the Life of John G. Paton.* Audio cd. Minneapolis: Desiring God Ministries, 2000.

Piper, William. Interview by Author, Easely, South Carolina, 07 July 2003.

Reapsome, Jim. "People Groups: Beyond the Push to Reach Them Lie Some Contrary Opinions." *Evangelical Missions Quarterly* 20 (January 1984): 6–19.

Reichenbach, Bruce R. *Evil and a Good God.* New York: Fordham University Press, 1982.

Robinson, William Childs. "Reconciliation." In *Baker's Dictionary of Theology*, ed., Everett F. Harrison, 437–38. Grand Rapids: Baker, 1960.

Robinson, Jeff. "Study: Recent Grads 3 Times More Likely to be Calvinist." In *Baptist Press* (November 27, 2007) . <http://www.bpnews.net/bpnews.asp?id=26914>. Accessed on 29 January 2010.

Saayman, Willem, and Klippies Kritzinger, eds. *Mission in Bold Humility: David Bosch's Works Considered.* Maryknoll, NY: Orbis, 1996.

Sayers, Dorothy. *A Matter of Eternity.* Grand Rapids: Eerdmans, 1973.

Serampore Compact. Quoted in Tom Ascol, "Calvinism, Evangelism & Founders Ministries." *Founders Journal* (Summer 2001), 1-21.

Smith, David. "The Church Growth Principles of Donald McGavran." *Transformation* 2, no. 2 (April/June 1985): 26.

Sovereign Grace Ministries. "Church Planting Frequently Asked Questions," In "*Sovereign Grace Ministries.*" http://www.SovereignGraceMinistries.org/ChurchPlanting/ChurchPlantingFAQ.aspx#08. Accessed on 3 February 2010.

_____. "We Plant & Build Local Churches with the Gospel: 2009-2010 Mission Update," In "*Sovereign Grace Ministries.*" <http://www.sovgracemin.org/Reference/MinistryBrochure%20web.pdf>. Accessed on 3 February 2010.

_____. "Who We Are," In "*Sovereign Grace Ministries.*" http://www.sovgracemin.org/About/AboutUs.aspx. Accessed on 3 February 2010.

Sproul, R. C. "Pelagianism," Renewing Your Mind. June 1996. Tape of the Month, *Ligonier Ministries*, 1996. Audio cd.

Spurgeon, Charles. "The Early Years, 1834–1859." In *Autobiography*. Revised, edited and complied by Susannah Spurgeon and Joseph Harrald. Vol. 1 . Edinburgh: Banner of Truth, 1962. Reprint, 1994.

Stewart, Kenneth J. "Calvinism and Missions: The Contested Relationship Revisited." In *Themelios* 34, no. 1 (April 2009), <http://www.thegospelcoalition.org/publications/34-1/calvinismand-missions-the-contested-relationship-revisited/#a29>. Accessed on 22 January 2010.

Strong, A. H. *Systematic Theology*. Westwood, NJ: Revell, 1907.

Sweatman, Kent Ellis. "The Doctrines of Calvinism in the Preaching of Charles Haddon Spurgeon." Ph.D. diss., Southwestern Baptist Theological Seminary, 1998.

Synod of Dort. In *Calvin College*. <http://www.ccel.org/creeds/canonsof-dort.html>. Accessed 26 August 2003.

The Desiring God Staff, "What Does John Piper Mean When He Says That He Is a 'Seven Point' Calvinist?" In "*Desiring God Ministries.*" <http://desiringgod.org/library/theologicalqa/calvinism/seven_points.html>. Accessed 2 September 2003.

The London Baptist Confession of 1644. In *Phillip Johnson*. <http://www.gty.org/~phil/creeds/bc1 644.htm>. Accessed 27 December 2002.

The Westminister Confession of 1646. In "*Center for Reformed Theology and Apologetics.*" <http://www.reformed.org/documents/westminster_conf_of_faith. html#chap14>. Accessed 23 January 2003.

Tippett, A. R., ed. *God, Man and Church Growth*. Grand Rapids: Eerdmans, 1973.

Toon, Peter. *The Emergence of Hyper-Calvinism in English Nonconformity, 1689–1765*. London: Olive Tree, 1967.

Tucker, Ruth A. *From Jerusalem to Irian Jaya: A Biographical History of Christian Missions*. Grand Rapids: Academie, 1983.

Warfield, Benjamin Breckinridge. *Calvin and Calvinism*. New York: Oxford University Press, 1931.

_____. *Calvin as a Theologian and Calvinism Today: Three Addresses in Commemoration of the Four-Hundredth Anniversary of the Birth of John Calvin*. Philadelphia: Presbyterian Board of Publications, 1909.

Winter, Ralph. "3 Men, 3 Eras: The Flow of Missions." *Mission Frontiers* 3, no 2 (Feb 1 981), 1-7.

_____. "Four Men, Three Eras." *Mission Frontiers* 19 (Nov 1 997),11-18.

_____."The Concept of a Third Era in Missions." *EMQ,* 17, no 2 (April 1981), 72.

Vance, Laurence M. *The Other Side of Calvinism.* Pensacola, FL: Vance Publications, 1999.

Verkuyl, Johannes. "The Biblical Foundation for the Worldwide Mission Mandate." In Ralph D. *Winter and Steven C. Hawthorne, eds., Perspectives* on the World Christian Movement: *A Reader.* Pasadena, CA: William Carey Library, 1992, 49-63.

_____. "My Pilgrimage in Mission." *International Bulletin of Missionary Research* 10 no. 4 (October 1, 1986), 150-153.

Veith, Gene Edward. "The Century's Top 100 Books." In *World on the Web* 14 no. 47 <http://www.worldmag.com/world/issue/12-04-99/cover_1 .asp>. Accessed on 24 March 2003.

Wayland, Francis, ed. *Memoir of the Life and Labor of the Rev. Adoniram Judson, D.D.* 2 Vols. Boston: Phillips, Sampson, & Co., 1835.

Westminster Confession of Faith (1646). In *Center for Reformed Theology and Apologetics.* <http://www.reformed.org/documents/westminster_conf_of_faith.html#chap3>. Accessed 22 August 2003.

Wilson, Christy, J. *Apostle to Islam: A Biography of Samuel M. Zwemer.* New York: Friendship Press, 1970.

"Who is Desiring God." In *"Desiring God Ministries."* <http://www.desiringgod.org/who_is_dgm_index .html>. Accessed 24 November 2004.

Williams, Sam. "The Justification of God." *Journal of Biblical Literature* 104 (Spring 1 985): 548–51.

Winter, Ralph D. "Four Men, Three Eras, Two Transitions: Modern Missions." In *Perspectives on the World Christian Movement: A Reader*, eds. Ralph D. Winter and Steven C. Hawthrone,

Wright, N. T. "The Justification of God." *Evangelical Quarterly* 60 (January 1988): 80–84.

Yamamori, Tetsunao, and Charles R. Taber, eds. *Christopaganism or Indigenous Christianity*. South Pasadena, CA: William Carey Library, 1975.

Zwemer, Samuel. "Calvinism and the Missionary Enterprise." *Theology Today* 7, no. 2 (July 1 950), 206-21.

Milton Keynes UK
Ingram Content Group UK Ltd.
UKHW030712041024
449263UK00001B/108

9 781631 999147